Does This Town Have Water?

by

Shaun Pinchbeck

William Sessions Limited
The Ebor Press
York, England

ISBN 1 85072 230 7

Printed in 11 on 12 point Plantin typeface
by Sessions of York
The Ebor Press
York, England

Introduction

AUGUST 1989: Offices of Heptonstalls, Solicitors, Goole, Humberside.

'Is there anything else we need to know?'

'I think I should let you know that in December I am planning to go to South America.'

'Oh, that shouldn't be a problem. We can work round holidays.'

'I see. Only it's not what you'd normally call . . . a holiday.'

The partners' brows furrowed.

'I'm actually planning on going for six months.'

Silence.

'So you mean you're wanting to work for ten weeks, then have six months off?'

'That's right.'

More furrowing of brows.

'We were really looking for someone who was going to stay a little longer.'

It seemed I'd blown this interview big time. A speedy recovery was called for.

'If it's any help, I'll commit myself to return to you after the six months.'

It was, and I did.

I remain indebted to my then employers (now my partners) for showing such patience.

I also thank Jo for hers. That patience was required for this trip will soon become clear to you.

Finally, I thank you, the reader, for buying this book. Enjoy!

Shaun Pinchbeck, Bubwith

To the memory of my grandmother,

and to Mari and Katri

Chapter 1

I HAD A NEIGHBOUR.

Sometimes conversations on aeroplanes, as on other forms of transport, just seem to flow from the outset. On other occasions, and on every occasion in the case of the London Underground, whole journeys pass in silence. This plane ride was showing all the signs of falling into the second category.

I contemplated what I had left behind; the English winter, steady work, real ale and, hardest of all, Jo. The first two I could do without, the third I would have to do without, and Jo, who I could not easily do without, would at least be joining me in another month.

Around the time the plane left England's coastline, I started Paul Theroux's *The Old Patagonian Express*. It is the story of a train ride from Massachusetts to Argentina and was designed to expunge at least some of my ignorance about the Continent into which I would arrive tomorrow. My neighbour was also reading. Occasionally we glanced up at the same time and caught each other's eye but just as quickly glanced away again.

It was when supper arrived and reading material had to be temporarily discarded that conversation became imminent. I think it started with our agreeing on the quality of aeroplane food, a fairly safe topic for starters unless you happen to be one of that rare breed of people who actually enjoys it. It was immediately apparent that my neighbour was not.

It emerged that he had become disillusioned with medicine and Manchester and particularly the hours he was required to work,

1

and had chucked it all in to teach English in Madrid. Madrid, he informed me, had an extraordinary night life resulting in regular traffic jams at 3.00 am. There did not otherwise appear to be anything very remarkable about it.

In no time we were there. There was certainly nothing remarkable about Madrid airport, and although it was late, two hours was insufficient to sample the night life. It was to be a two hour wait for the connecting flight to Rio de Janeiro, a city of which I knew nothing except that it is the capital of Brazil which I was shortly to discover it in fact is not.

The wait passed quickly thanks to Derek. He spoke English fluently but with an accent I could not recognise.

"Where are you from?" I asked.

"Brazil," he replied.

"I am returning home, I have been six years in London working in bars and that kind of thing and touring Europe. It is time to go home."

I told him he was the first Brazilian I had ever met.

"There are masses of Brazilians in London. They are all working in the bars and restaurants getting paid peanuts."

He must have detected my ignorance for he proved to be a mine of information about Brazil. He stressed the dangers, particularly in Rio – a lot of thieving – and tried to explain about the currency. The currency had been the Cruzeiro but this soon became so weak that the Cruzado had been introduced, worth 1,000 Cruzeiros. That did nothing to stem the tide of inflation and so the new Cruzado had recently been brought in, worth 1,000 Cruzados.

"You've got to grasp it or they will rip you off."

Hard though it was at 1.00 am, my financial resources were sufficiently meagre to ensure that these details would not be forgotten.

The plane from Madrid was almost full. I had been very lucky to be on it. Well over a month earlier, admittedly later than I should have been arranging it, it had been the only available flight before Christmas. "It's all the Brazilians in England going home for Christmas," said the travel agent. "What Brazilians in England?" I had thought. This plane load was the answer.

It was about a 12 hour flight largely spent endeavouring to sleep, unfortunately with little or no success. On arrival, Derek ensured that I obtained the new Cruzados rather than the Cruzeiros and, with greater ease than would have been the case had I been solely responsible, we found the stop for the bus to central Rio. There was a timetable. Derek warned that Brazilian timetables tend to be at best a guide and at worst a figment of someone's imagination, and so it proved. The 9.25 failed to materialise. The 9.55 which wasn't due to materialise, did, but was going somewhere which didn't appear on any timetable and finally the 10.25 pulled in on time. It seemed too good to be true, and indeed it was. It remained there for 15 minutes without explanation. Finally, the driver got out and started bashing the back of the bus with a hammer. Derek shrugged his shoulders and said, "Welcome to Brazil." Finally at around 11.00 am we left.

After his warnings and because of his fluency in English and Portuguese and my deficiencies in Portuguese, I had taken the liberty of asking if I could go with him into Rio where he was visiting a friend. Fortunately, not only because I felt much safer but also because he knew a lot about Rio, he had agreed.

The airport is some 20 miles up the coast from Central Rio. The northern part of Rio is largely inhabited by blacks, descendants of the African slaves imported into Brazil in the last century because the Indians were considered either too lazy or too drunk to work. The accommodation is cramped; many sleep in the streets. It is a part of Rio which tourists will probably only see twice, on the way to, and on the way from, the airport. The only "attraction" in the north is the Maracana Soccer Stadium, built for the 1956 World Cup and the World's largest with a capacity of 200,000. Derek explained that the city's name is Portuguese for, "River of January". It was discovered by a Portuguese explorer on New Years Day 1502 and he had somehow mistaken the city's vast bay for a river.

We left the northern zone and came into the area known as Central. This is the business area and a considerable improvement. There we stopped and took a taxi to "Jardim Botanique", which, in addition to a botanical garden, also takes in a residential area. It was here that Derek's friends lived. He had not seen them for some time and there was a good deal of back slapping, hugging and laughter. I felt a bit of a prune.

3

However, they welcomed me in. The television was showing pictures of what appeared to be a huge crowd of football supporters. The screen was filled with a mass of bodies waving banners and flags, singing and cheering. I knew from my viewing of World Cups that football in Brazil was, to quote the late Bill Shankly, "not a matter of life and death but much more important than that". "You're fanatical on football here aren't you?"

"Oh this isn't football," Derek replied, "this is the Presidential election campaign."

The Election was due to be held on Sunday week, in nine days time. It was to be Brazil's first Election for some 30 years. There were two candidates: a slick, slim, youthful and apparently extremely wealthy 40 year old by the name of Collar for the right and a chubby, bearded, charmless looking character by the name of Lula, who, despite appearances, was marginally younger, for the left.

Lula boasted proudly of his working class roots. His main claim to fame appeared to be that as a factory worker he had once lost a few fingers in an industrial accident. He hoped to appeal to the hearts and souls of Brazilians, of whom there were evidently many, who led a life of struggle, under paid, or even unpaid, and trampled on, whilst the likes of Collar and his cronies enjoyed a life of luxury without appearing to have to do much for it. It was, in short, the classic struggle of left versus right.

Collar was clearly ahead in the polls. However, there were allegations that he had sufficient resources, both in funds and in friends, to be able, amongst other activities, to hand out copies of ballot papers showing a cross by his name. It must be remembered that a high percentage of Brazilians are illiterate. They could not appreciate the difference between the rival dogmas but they could copy the position of a cross.

I went to Rio with the phone number of a friend of a work colleague of Jo's. It was a tenuous link but I called him and he said we must have a beer. I liked the sound of that. He would come and collect me. Even better. The flight had taken its toll on Derek, as it had done on me earlier, and he was out for the count on the sofa. I left him a message to hopefully see him in his own town of Porto Allegre. I thanked his friends for their hospitality – they had provided food, bathroom, a sofa to sleep on and a T.V., and had received very little in return beyond a shattered Englishman's first tentative and ill informed impressions of their country – and departed with Paul.

Paul had lived in Rio for two years and loved it. This may have had something to do with the fact that he hailed from Reading. His driving appeared fast and lane changing frequent. "People drive like maniacs here," he said as he drove some distance down the wrong side of the road to take a turning without any sign of an indication. We got stuck in traffic. Horns honked for no apparent reason. Young barefooted boys of seven or eight walked down the road between cars offering pieces of mango and sweets to frustrated drivers. "They will sell anything here and at any time," Paul told me.

We were driving around a large lake called the Lagoa, a man made lake in the heart of the more salubrious part of Rio dividing Jardim Botanique from Ipanema and Copacabana. It is about two miles long by a mile wide. It seemed remarkable in a city of around six million inhabitants that so much prime space could remain untapped. It was an encouraging sign – rather like the Padang cricket ground in the centre of Singapore's business district – that the city kept things in perspective. It had not gone too crazy in the urge or the pressure to develop.

Within half an hour we had reached Ipanema and were sitting outside a bar soaking up the sun.
"What will you have'?" Paul asked.
"Whatever you recommend, preferably something typically Brazilian."
"Right," he said licking his lips.

He ordered a beer for himself and what I later discovered was a Caipirhini for me. Caipirhini is the national drink. It comprises crushed ice and fresh squeezed and unsqueezed limes and a beverage prepared to a secret Brazilian recipe but most closely compared to Vodka. Indeed it is possible to use Vodka instead. It is then called, rather originally, a Caipivodka. It was both refreshing and delicious. It was only an hour or so later, after a couple more and having tried to stand up, that its strength became apparent.

"It's a good life here," Paul explained, "the sun shines, there are beaches galore, so many restaurants and bars, you have a flat provided, a maid to keep it clean, the company provides a car and everything is so cheap. You can live like a king."

Paul was part of a group of about 20 English men and women who worked for Ferranti. There were, I discovered, in the region of 10,000 British living in Rio. Perhaps the best known amongst them is Ronald Biggs who had recently thrown a party for anyone who is anyone in Rio to celebrate his 60th birthday.

"How do you fancy coming to a stag night tonight?" Paul asked me. He had briefly mentioned it on the phone and this was probably something that had slipped out under the influence of the sun and the beer. Despite hardly having slept for about 40 hours I did not feel tired.

"There will be a big crowd of us, mainly English, my girlfriend's coming as well." Never having turned down a stag night before, it seemed inappropriate to do so in Rio.

We went back to Paul's flat a few minutes away. He had told me his girlfriend – in fact his fiance – would be there. She could not speak much English although she spoke some French. The flat was on the 8th floor and had a view of the Plaza General Osario and, if you craned your neck a bit, of Ipanema beach. It could only have been 100 yards away. Christina had a lively, attractive and cheerful face and a solid build which I was to discover was a feature of many Brazilian girls. We spoke briefly in French but it soon emerged that her English was at least as adequate as my French and reverted to it. This had the advantage that Paul could also join in the conversation.

"You can stay here tonight," Paul offered, "there is a spare room." This came as something of a relief. The speed with which so much had happened, and the Caipirhini, had combined, I think, to lead me to temporarily overlook the practicalities, namely the need to find somewhere to stay and then to return to it alone at what was likely to be a late hour in an unfamiliar and apparently dangerous city. Thankfully that would not now be necessary.

We walked to a Chinese Restaurant in the Plaza General Osario. A crowd of Englishmen were at a long table interspersed with one Brazilian chap and several Brazilian girls who were the Englishmen's girlfriends. It came as a bit of a shock to discover that one of the girls was actually the bride.

A mass of food appeared: plates of crisp vegetables, chicken chow mein, shredded beef, cashews, water chestnuts and bowls of rice. At one point I wondered if it would ever stop coming. I had a delicious orange juice, not an English version but literally the juice of freshly squeezed oranges, and a few more glasses of Caipirhini. It seemed to be a no expense spared occasion. The bill came to £3 per head.

Afterwards we headed to a bar just over the road from Copacabana beach. More Englishmen turned up, a few in fancy dress although I never fathomed out why. They all seemed very chummy. There was obviously a "young English set" or perhaps there were several such sets and this was just one of them. A few of them persuaded me to join them in a night club by the name of "Help". As I had by then knocked back some more Caipirhinis, they had not had a difficult task.

Once inside, the combination of the heat inside it, the alcohol inside me and the lack of sleep suddenly proved too much. Despite the best efforts of a scantily clad local girl – I remained awake just long enough to appreciate that this was no ordinary night club – I was quickly asleep. It was 4.00 am when I awoke. "Help" seemed in full swing. It took a while to take in all that had happened. How exactly did I come to be in a night club full of prostitutes at 4.00 am on my first night in this wholly unfamiliar city with not a clue of how to find my temporary home?

Chapter 2

SUBSEQUENT DAYS passed more sensibly. Paul and Christina very kindly offered my their spare room until Christmas. The first week was largely spent trying to find a job.

I had undertaken this trip intending it to be a six month tour of South, and then Central, America squeezing in the West coast of the United States and Vancouver, Canada, at the end. The idea was born, blossomed and finally came to fruition during two years as an articled clerk with a firm of solicitors in Bath. Six months seemed to be the minimum period to do it justice. There was the rather significant problem of money. In a nutshell the problem was that I didn't have any.

Being an articled clerk is hardly conducive to saving, nor, with its plethora of restaurants and watering holes, is living in Bath. The combination was deadly. I would have to leave. I would go up north where I knew nobody, the rent would be low and I would go into temporary seclusion. There cannot be many firms of solicitors or indeed any employer who would take on a person who says he wants to work for ten weeks and then take a six months holiday. I was fortunate to find one that did, in Goole, where indeed I remain.

I set off with £1,500 in travellers cheques. This would have to last six months. Hence the need for work. The obvious source was English language schools: I got through some shoe leather hunting them out but it was the same story each time: just breaking up for Christmas although really you need a permit anyway. I tried journalism: there had been an English language newspaper but it was the inspiration of one lady and when she died so did it.

Law firms were sympathetic but could not see how I could assist without knowing the language. Disappointing though this was, I could not see any way of disagreeing. After a week or more of searching, a Brazilian lady said to me, "Forget it, do as the Cairocas do and go to the beach, its Christmas time, nobody works now." Reluctantly in one way although not in another I followed her advice.

Going to the beach in Rio is not quite like going to the beach anywhere else. The phrase, "life is a beach", which you can sometimes see on the T shirts of people who probably haven't been near one for years, could not apply to anywhere more than to Rio. Life revolves around it. The city has over 40 miles of beaches. One beach alone, at San Conrada in the south, is 15 miles long. Imagine it: a walk of four hours to go from one end to the other.

Nowadays the most popular and best known beaches are those of Copacabana and Ipanema. You can quite easily be left wondering whether anyone in Rio actually does any work. They are a nearly permanent hive of activity. Distractions are everywhere. The bikini, born in Rio, still flourishes, as do most to whose bodies it clings. Little is left to the imagination. When it all gets too much you can join throngs of bare footed joggers and when the heat knocks you out, which in my case was shortly after starting, you can take to the waters where the waves will have the same effect. Every now and again, battered and bruised like a prize fighter, you will time a dive to perfection and body surf to the shore and it will all seem worthwhile. I spent many happy afternoons on the ropes of the sea looking for the knock out punch.

The activity and energy of Ipanema beach, my personal favourite, never ceased to amaze. There were always people doing sit ups on the benches or pulling themselves up on the bars which had been constructed in the sand, and several games of volleyball were generally taking place at any time. Every afternoon you could admire a display – for that was how it seemed – of natural talent, flair and touch as the locals played soccer on their temporary pitches in the sand. Had our boys not snatched it from them in 1966, Brazil would have won the World Cup four consecutive times. It was easy to see why, and hard to see how they have failed by their own high standards in the past two decades.

It may be that Brazilian soccer is a microcosm of the country: exciting, energetic, attacking and full of flair and individual skills but ultimately let down perhaps by a lack of team work and a suspect

9

defence. Caution and security are not words that spring to mind when thinking of Brazilian soccer, nor of the country as a whole.

There was never a dull moment and there need never be an idle one. Energy could be restored by sampling the huge variety of sandwiches, nuts, yogurts, juices and ice cream to name but a few items regularly on tap from the beach vendors. Bliss for me at the end of a day on Ipanema beach was a coconut, recently plucked from a palm tree on the beach and kept cool in a basin of refrigerated water. Out it would come, green and vast and nearly round, the water splashing from it. A local vendor, holding it at the bottom in one hand, would cut it open at the top with a knife of a thickness and sharpness normally reserved for meat. Four cuts in quick succession and somehow always the same depth and symmetrical would leave a small hole for a straw and there it was; natural, fresh, slightly thick and sweet, not to say a little nutty, it was quite irresistible and so I found was another . . . and another. And even when, after a lot of noisy sucking and moving of the straw around the inside of the nut, you finally had to admit defeat and accept that the juice was at an end, all was still not lost. Four more sharp cuts to the side and the nut was cracked open, the white insides ready to be devoured.

Rio is more than just beaches. Its most famous landmark is a vast statue of Christ, 130 feet tall and weighing 1,200 tons. Standing as it does, arms outstretched on the peak of a 2,000 feet mountain by the name of Corcovado, it can be seen from almost anywhere in Rio and quite literally embraces the city. I took a train from central Rio which ascended slowly and steeply through forest and suddenly rose beyond it to produce a quite stunning panoramic view of the beaches, mountains, islands and of course skyscrapers of Rio. There can be few more spectacular views of a city anywhere in the world. Once at the top there was a chance to wander and admire from all angles. You could happily spend an entire day there. The statue, which from ground level looked like a small human being, now appeared, to steal an over used Americanism, "quite awesome". The head alone is the equivalent height of three people standing on top of each other. Even the floodlights, which ensure that it never loses its grip on Rio and its inhabitants, are overwhelming in their magnitude.

From the top of the Corcovado you can clearly see Rio's other great landmark – the Sugar Loaf. Whereas the Corcovado is set back some miles from the beaches, the Sugar Loaf, a vast granite cone, rises 1,200 feet directly above the water. The journey up the Sugar Loaf is by cable car. This is not a trip for the faint hearted, although it is mildly surprising, and very comforting, to know that there has never been an accident. The reward is a quite magnificent view of the city of Rio and its beaches and islands and has the advantage over the Corcovado that Christ is also in view looking down on his paradise.

Facing the Brazilians at Maracana Stadium. (I tipped it over the bar.)

Chapter 3

YOU MAY BE MISTAKEN for thinking that I fell in love with Rio. From the top of the Corcovado or the Sugar Loaf or on the beaches you could think that your search for paradise was at an end. Sadly there is another side to the paradise: much of Rio's population is desperately poor.

It appears largely to be those of African origin imported as slaves in the last century by European settlers. The lucky ones live in shanty towns of wooden hovels perched on hills thought too precarious to build on. The less fortunate sleep in the streets. Begging is commonplace. Often it is done by children as young as four or five.

I saw children enter restaurants and beg diners to part with some of their food. Sometimes they were hounded out by angry waiters, their bellies left aching. The lucky ones may be given some leftovers. I saw a boy of perhaps six years roll up his shirt for a diner to empty the remains of his plate into it. He took it outside and shared it with a few friends. I have heard suggestions that these poor and desperate children are periodically shot dead as they are bad for tourism. Out of sheer desperation, I suspect, many for whom a meal would be a rare luxury resort to other methods if begging fails. The most usual and most talked about amongst the English is the production of a knife.

On 30th December, the day on which I finally left the comfort and security of Paul and Christina's flat and the first occasion therefore when I had to travel in Rio with some luggage, I was sitting in a square in a region called Catete taking a rest during a search for accommodation. It was 10 o'clock in the morning and the streets were busy. It was very hot – perhaps 100° – and I took my shirt off.

Although supposedly still hidden by my shorts, it seems, with the benefit of hindsight, that my money belt was thus revealed.

A minute or so later I felt a tug from behind. I turned sharply. A large black man with alternate teeth was standing over me. He had his arm out and said something in Portuguese. I told him I did not understand (which in a sense was true). No matter how much you feel you should give, it is a dangerous thing to do. Firstly, you reveal where your money is and secondly you will have the whole neighbourhood onto you. I shook my head. Sometimes they would then go away.

This one did not. He did not look very friendly. I thought I should move away. I stood up and took a few steps and suddenly a knife was at my throat. Everything happened so quickly. No sooner had the knife appeared than it had gone again. Unfortunately so too had my bag and money belt. I stood in this busy street. Almost everyone was black. It was hopeless. In a flash my possessions were gone.

When I had even a few seconds to pause, I realised that I had actually been robbed by a boy, the alternate tooth wonder's accomplice, who could not have been much more than eight years old. It was also only then that I could take in that the knife, far from being one that could have sliced through a human throat or even a slab of meat in a split second, was only the size of an ordinary kitchen knife, in fact not only was it the size of one it actually was one.

This was not a touristy area; nobody would speak English. I had other feelings beside one of utter helplessness: anger with myself at letting it happen, for sitting and thoughtlessly removing my shirt, but the other feeling, and a surprising one perhaps, was one of relief, not just at keeping body intact but at actually experiencing being robbed at knife point.

Whenever I had met British people during the three weeks preceding this incident they had warned me of the risks; don't wear a watch or go out at night alone or take the buses or reveal a camera. I had been cautious at first but as time passed without a problem inevitably a feeling that the risk had been exaggerated came over me and I was left wondering: how do they rob you? How does it feel to be confronted with a knife or even as sometimes happens a gun? The fear of the unknown was almost greater than the fear when it happened. That is how it was in fact a relief. It was also a relief to have had so little on me: £2 in cash for the hotel and a few clothes. I had Paul to thank for insisting that valuables remained in his flat.

I would have to report it; this may take some time and the Police would want to know when it happened. I should make a note of the time. It was only then that I realised that it wasn't just my bag and money they had got but my watch had gone too. This was an unnerving discovery – rendered almost naked in a split second, the full extent of the appropriation only dawning gradually. I really had very little left: in fact a pair of shorts and a pair of sandals. What a sorry state of affairs! How terribly wrong it had all suddenly turned. I wanted to go home.

This thought lasted about ten seconds. I reported the theft to a local hotel and after the sort of frustration you get when giving a clue in charades which is blindingly obvious but which nobody can get and having then waited about an hour, the Police finally arrived. Despite being called the "Tourist Police", they had not a word of English between them.

"I do not speak good Portuguese," I told them in an accent which must have proved the point. "If you take me to Ipanema (about 15 minutes drive away) my friend will translate for you."

"We can't do that."

"Why?"

"It's not our area."

"But it's very near."

"Not allowed."

"Can the Ipanema Police take me there?"

"No, they are only in Ipanema, they can't come here."

"But surely you have to sometimes cross areas."

"No, impossible."

This was unbearable, every bit as painful as the theft itself. I nabbed passers by in desperation and spilled out the story. They looked at me with sympathy.

This is incredible," I said to one.

"No," he replied, "this is Brazil."

I finally persuaded the officers of the Catete constabulary to part with the princely sum of five pence for my bus fare to Ipanema. "You won't believe what's happened," I said to Paul, "but I have

14

been robbed." His lack of reaction suggested that he had no difficulty at all in believing it.

"What with?" he asked.

"A knife," I replied.

"It was bound to happen, it happens to everyone, with me it was a gun."

So I had made the grade – free life membership of the exclusive (although not too exclusive) "Robbed in Rio" club.

It transpired that 30th December 1989 was the most depressing day of the whole trip. I looked at everyone as a potential robber and had a miserable time seeking accommodation for a few pounds a night in Ipanema. This, I soon realised, was the equivalent of going for dinner at the Savoy and saying that you have only got a fiver. I ended up on a dusty mattress on the floor of a building site intended in due course to become a Youth Hostel. I hated Rio that night. What a disgusting filthy, noisy, crowded, unfriendly city. The rich are smug and the poor are robbers. Yuk! If finding accommodation in South America is going to be like this the trip will be a nightmare. Jo will never speak to me again.

It says something about Rio that 31st December 1989 was one of the most memorable; millions of happy jolly smiling faces on Copacabana beach as a firework display stretching for miles saw a new decade unleashed upon us. It was every inch of the way worthy of it and I felt that there could be fewer more exciting and fun places to be. It was all about celebration, fun, humour, spontaneity, noise and colour. The Brazilians are hard to beat on an occasion like that and Copacabana beach was a wonderful setting. How I loved Rio that night.

For me that is Rio in a nutshell. It is a city of extremes. It inspires and it can be loved. It infuriates and frightens and can be hated: I do not think that you could feel indifferent to it.

Chapter 4

JO ARRIVED ON 3RD JANUARY 1990. I could not wait to see her. Varig – the Brazilian airline – ensured that I had to. The flight was three hours late. After a month it took a while to return to each other's wave length but by supper time I think we had done it. I was inwardly very excited at the thought of being with her for five months but suspect that this may not have been entirely obvious to her. We spent 10 days in Rio and our voyage then began. Just as the day leaving Paul and Christina's flat proved troublesome, so did the day of departure from Rio.

We rushed madly to catch the 11.00 o'clock coast road bus south to Santos only to find there was no place, then somehow missed out on the 1.00 pm as well and finally got the 3.00 pm which then didn't take the coast road. I stuffed my sleeping bag under a seat at the bus terminal to hide it from potential thieves and managed to hide it from myself as well. For all I know it could still be there. Six hours along a main road later we were in Santos. I can remember little about Brazil's largest port beyond the prostitutes outside our hotel and the reasonable beach nearby at San Vicente.

There was nothing to delay us in taking the few hours bus ride to Sao Paulo. Rio and Sao Paulo are the Brazilian equivalent of Edinburgh and Glasgow or Sydney and Melbourne. The inhabitants of one tend to dislike those of the other and speak badly of them. The Cairocas will tell you that Sao Paulo doesn't have the beaches, that it's huge and sprawling and that the people are serious. Our three days there did nothing to disprove their opinion. Perhaps, in a sprawling beachless city of 15 million people, there is little room for fun.

Sao Paulo residents, on the other hand, consider that Cairocas are lazy and perhaps even a little stupid, views with which I would also find it hard to argue. The three days were very relaxed and fun and fairly alcoholic, having, as we did, the good fortune to stay with Monica, a friend of a friend of mine. Monica did not find Sao Paulo too awful and seemed to tolerate the dangers, less serious perhaps than Rio but ever present nevertheless. Her house was surrounded by a 29 feet high wall with nails and broken glass on the top to deter potential burglars. Many other large houses resembled top security prisons from the outside.

We visited Curitiba, six hours by bus south of Sao Paulo, to take a train journey reputed to be the loveliest in Brazil. Curitiba was in many ways a breath of fresh air. It was modern and prosperous, beggars were not in evidence and its people seemed friendly, alert and well dressed. There was an overall impression of space – enhanced by several pedestrianised areas – sadly seldom felt in a big city. More European than either Rio or Sao Paulo, it was hard to believe that at 1.5 million it had a population larger than any British city bar London.

The train journey to the port of Paranagua was disappointing. True, it rose several thousand feet and took us along a winding track around and alongside mountains and waterfalls and was at times quite spectacular, but my undying memory is of broccoli trees. I do not know what they actually were, but if broccoli grew on trees then that is what they would look like, and broccoli is hardly the most exciting of vegetables. Our expectations had perhaps been too high and certainly it could not be faulted for value. The four hour journey set us back the princely sum of 80 pence each.

My other memory of Curitiba is that we stayed in a brothel. Not intentionally, I hasten to add, although perhaps the price of our double room with private bathroom, the same as the train tickets, should have been a clue. Our suspicions were raised when for no apparent reason we were moved to a different room and all but confirmed when the Chinese owner said that ours was being used for "massage". All doubt was removed by the subsequent presence in and around our old room of what can only be described as a harem of women in bathing costumes.

We spent an entire day on a bus heading West from Curitiba to the town of Foz do Iguaçu.* It was well out of our way but there was a reason.

When President Roosevelt's wife saw the Iguazu* Falls she is reported to have commented, "Poor poor Niagara". How can such a household name be compared so unfavourably to one barely even heard of outside its own countries? I say countries because the Iguazu Falls lie in both Brazil and Argentina.

"Start on the Brazil side," we were told, "for the best general views then go over to Argentina to be right in the thick of it." We followed the advice and the view pretty quickly took our breath away.

Torrents of water powered down in no less than 275 falls over a frontage of one and half miles. It was nothing short of phenomenal. We stood and stared, mesmerised.

Sometime later, a coach pulled up and a group of 20 or so Japanese climbed out. They were cheerful and smiling, in that Japanese way. They walked towards us and we watched in hopeful expectation of that wonderful look of excitement and bewilderment which the Japanese have mastered the art of displaying. We were to be disappointed. Before reaching a position where they could do justice to the view they had turned, with such precision timing that it looked rehearsed, lined up in two rows and had their photograph taken several times by one of their number.

Worse was to come. The group then moved off without even a glance in the direction of Argentina. The photographs were not merely preceding their viewing of the Falls, they were actually replacing it. The truth dawned. They had not come to see the Falls; they had come to be photographed in front of them. No doubt they had to hurry off for the next "tourist site". I saw in those seconds why people can rebel against photography whilst travelling.

The Argentinian side did not have the views but you could walk precariously along slippery planks of wood between the Falls, feel the spray and both hear and sense the power. It was here that a scene in *The Mission* was filmed.

It had been something of a detour inland to the Iguazu Falls and a night bus took us back to the coast at Porto Allegre. The Cairocas had been fairly disparaging about this town and port of

---

* The spelling alters in translation.

Christ embracing
Rio de Janeiro.

Aerial view of Rio.

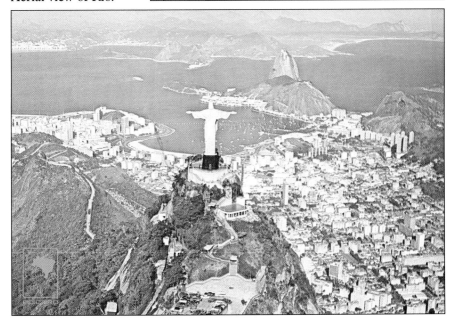

A fairly typical Brazilian shower.

Ipanema Beach.

La Boca, Italian section of Buenos Aires.

Buenos Aires.

Shaun and Jo at Iguazu Falls.

Montevideo, Uruguay.

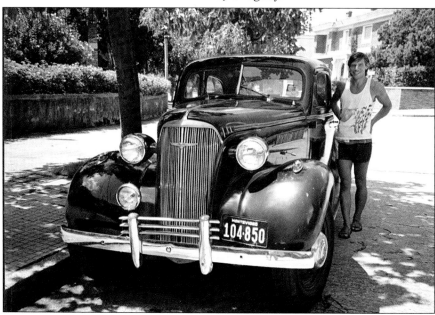

well over one million inhabitants, and the general view seemed to be that it was fairly dangerous, very boring and probably worth going out of your way to avoid. Derek was there and it was sort of on our way south so we gave it a day.

It was a pleasant surprise. A lot of Europeans, particularly Germans, Italians and English settled in and around Porto Allegre in the 19th century. The more salubrious areas looked how you might expect somewhere like Weybridge to look if blessed with a more generous climate. Leafy and spacious in a way that residential areas in Rio and Sao Paulo never seemed to be, you could imagine the people of Porto Allegre on a Sunday morning mowing the lawn, cleaning the car, going to the corner shop for papers, preparing a roast for lunch and decanting a few decent bottles from the local vineyard. It is only in this last respect that the comparison with Weybridge cannot be sustained.

"There are some very poor people in Porto Allegre as well," Derek explained, "but they seem to keep themselves to themselves. They are mainly black and live in the northern part of town and there isn't much mingling. It's safer than Rio in that respect."

In the evening in Porto Allegre we met an extremely vague contact of Jo's, by which I mean that the means of contact was vague because Marion was anything but. They had met in England only a few months before. Jo had overheard him mentioning that he lived in Brazil. They got chatting and he said that she must contact him if in Porto Allegre. He and his wife took us to a Churrascaria where unlimited quantities of meat stand upright on skewers in the middle of the table, to be devoured with salad and washed down with lager until the diners can take no more.

Mario entertained us with stories of his experiences of living in Rio, the United States, England, Italy, Germany and Buenos Aires. He spoke well of all nationalities except the Argentinians. His voice almost rose to fever pitch at the mere mention of them.

"Do you know what is the best business to have in Argentina?" he asked us.

We said we did not.

"You have a business buying Argentinians for what they are worth and selling them for what they think they are worth."

The next day we left Brazil. For me it was after seven weeks, for Jo after three. Despite many bus trips of 10 hours or so we had still only visited a tiny proportion of the country: a small part of the south east region. It was comparable to "seeing" England by visiting Hertfordshire, Essex and Kent, a trip for which seven weeks may seem excessive and which may give an impression less favourable than England deserves.

Sadly, we had had neither the time nor the finances to visit Brazil's most famous region; Amazonia. It lies in the north west of Brazil, some 3,000 miles from Porto Allegre. It boasts the world's largest and densest rain forest, the Amazonian Jungle, and the Amazon River which knocks statistical spots off even its nearest rival. Controversy surrounds the Brazilian Government's attempts to develop the area. Hordes of Brazilians from the North East, who may otherwise be unemployed, jump at the chance to earn a living cutting down the trees of Amazonia. There is worldwide condemnation of this destruction of the world's resources. For Brazil it is justified by the need to feed its ever rising population. What seems to annoy the Brazilians most is allegations that they have no concern for the environment. They point to the excessive car ownership in the States and in Europe and particularly the fact that their own vehicles run on alcohol. Suffice to say, there are vehemently held views on both sides, and the pages of his book are not the place to resolve them.

The most interesting thing about the border town was its name: Chui Chui. My only recollection is of the bread; a proper heavy loaf which I had not previously found in Brazil and which was hopefully a sign that, on the bread front at least, Uruguay would be an improvement.

Chapter 5

WE ENTERED URUGUAY in a bus. It could not have been easier, we did not even need to show our passports. The scenery was markedly different to that to which we had become accustomed in Brazil. The land was drier, the grass less lush, a yellow brown colour rather than green. It also seemed more fenced, more organised and less wild – was this difference to be limited to the scenery, I wondered. Visibility was wider, trees far less frequent, occasionally the road took a slight turn or dip but largely it was flat and straight. A few low lying hills could sometimes be seen in the distance and now and again we saw a cow or horse.

Sightings of humans were less frequent, and everytime they they were on bicycles. I recall being struck by this. There must have been very few cyclists in Brazil. Periodically we passed a village: the buildings were grey stone and brick and more solid looking than in the Brazilian villages. These villages were few and far between, very small and had no visible inhabitants.

After only a matter of hours we reached Maldonado. Maldonado is over half way along the south coast towards the capital Montevideo which in turn is over half way along the entire length of the south coast. It seemed odd, after the vast distances we had travelled in Brazil to do a journey which appeared inconsequential on the map, to have progressed over one quarter of the way along the south coast in a few hours. Uruguay is in fact roughly the same size as England and Wales but has under 3,000,000 inhabitants.

Our reason for stopping at Maldonado was to visit the nearby beach resort of Punta Del Este. It has a reputation for exclusivity and class; a popular hideaway a generation or two ago for the English aristocracy. The short bus journey from Maldonado took us through woods of luxury houses and shining BMWs. Punta Del

Este was at first sight slightly disappointing: the beach was quiet and expansive and the sea calm and clean, but it had fallen to the temptation of the high rise and there appeared to be nothing to particularly mark it out.

Our view altered in a beachside bar over some fresh fish and a drink. The sun was setting, the waiters polite and unobtrusive, the food fresh, tasty and attractively presented, the conversation quiet, slow, thoughtful and relaxing. Faces and bodies glowed with good health. It is hard to describe it but it is a feeling of being amongst people of quality knowing how to relax in an atmosphere conducive to it.

It was not an atmosphere which the Brazilians seemed quite able to create: they were just that little bit too loud and certainly the food was often short on taste and the service short on quality. We could see then why Punta Del Este had an appeal and an attraction: a million miles away from the pot bellies, red faces, fish and chip shops, amusements arcades and lager louts of all too many English beach resorts. I am too young to know if Punta Del Este is the England or part of the England of old, but if it is, where have we gone wrong, because there is surely no English Punta Del Este now.

In Maldonado we stayed at a hostel run by an Irishman in his fifties with the usual Irish twinkle in his eye. We stayed there because of him rather than the hostel which was to say the least run down. During the night it poured with rain and the roof leaked. In the morning several inches of water lay on the floor of the communal area and a few young girls were trying to mop it up.

"Is t'ere rain in your room?" he asked us.

"A little bit," I replied, understating considerably.

"Oh tat's O.K., te roof leaks," he informed us, displaying the Irish ability to state the obvious in a way that, despite the fact that he ran the place, suggested that really it was quite beyond his control or concern. "It should have been repaired last week but te chap didn't turn up."

He boiled some eggs for us, wading between our makeshift table and his makeshift kitchen, and asked us about our trip. "I suppose you are going to write a book about all this." He was the first person – and as it transpired the last – to say it.

He told us that he could write a book about this hostel. He had been there nine years. Uruguay, he informed us, is the "End of the World." It appeared, that after a divorce he wanted a fresh start, and took the rather drastic step of seeking it in Argentina. His venture there having failed, he moved next door to "The End of the World".

"I have had strange happenings in here, you know." We had already witnessed one; on arrival a lady had been waiting with us, or that is what I had thought until Jo asked me if I realised it was a man. "He or she or it or whatever you want to call him . . . or her," the Irishman explained, "is a man . . . about fifty and married. He comes here quite often and likes to put on breasts and dress as a woman. Last night he told my wife he was going to be unfaithful to his wife – with a man and asked my wife if 'he' or 'she' looked o.k."

He told us that a Paraguayan diplomat's wife had knocked on the door in the early hours of one morning accompanied by a black man, her chauffeur driven car outside, and asked for a room for half an hour. He charged her 30 US dollars and then saw her pay the black man 1,000 US dollars cash and wished he had charged a lot more.

Montevideo, a few hours bus ride west, dominates its country in a way few capitals can. It has nearly a third of the total population and, being on the coast with both the country's major port and several beaches, it is not only the country's trade centre but is also a major summer resort. It takes its name from the view of the city obtained by walking up the 350 feet high hill to the western end of the bay. Rio had perhaps spoilt us, for the view, whilst good, was certainly not spectacular.

Montevideo had long, sandy and not very busy beaches with relatively calm waters, some pleasant parks, a lot of vintage cars, a few attractive plazas, a run down and dirty old city and Heladerios. The last named – ice cream parlours – seemed to be something of an institution. About 25 flavours were on offer from the stodgy dulce de leche (literally sweet milk) to the more sorbet like lemon and peach. There were often 30 or so people per Heladerio sampling their favourite. Ice cream eating was clearly serious business, an art not to be rushed.

23

Montevideo and indeed Uruguay in general failed to invoke any strong feelings in either Jo or me. It seemed reasonably safe, quite pleasant, its people fairly friendly and the food at best average. Unlike Brazil, where there was much to love and sadly just as much to hate, Uruguay was just nondescript. Certainly it did not live up to its reputation of being the Switzerland of South America, unless Switzerland too has slums, filthy streets and people sleeping in them. Sadly, the "Golden Age" of Uruguay appears to be an end.

Chapter 6

THE JOURNEY TO BUENOS AIRES was diabolical. It could be undertaken either by bus round the River Plate, boat on the River Plate or a combination of the two. For no other reason than that it was the cheapest, we took the combination through the night. The bus at Montevideo, due to depart well before midnight, did not arrive until well after, and then we had the misfortune to sit above the back wheel thus absorbing the bumps which were all too frequent. How Jo managed to sleep through some of it I will never know; was there more to the ice creams than met the eye?

At 4.00 am the bus reached the connection point but we had to go through a further ordeal of queuing yet again to show our tickets and then we all staggered along, half asleep, before falling onto the hard upright wooden seats of a tiny cramped boat. At around 7.30 am, we landed at Tigre in Argentina, where it was standing room only on the one hour bus journey to the capital.

We were determined to judge Argentinians on their merits and not on the opinions of Brazilians and other travellers who had generally dismissed them as arrogant, lazy, heavy going and humourless. We were also determined to practice our Spanish, the language of all South and Central America with the exception of Brazil.

Marta, who we had met on the bus, gave us a chance to do both: a law student at Buenos Aires University who spoke hardly any English, she told us of the terrible state of her country: inflation is crippling, the people are losing heart and President Menhem appears to take more interest in football than politics and tends to leave the running of the country to his brother. It should have sounded grim but she said it in such a bubbly, interested way that it actually sounded rather exciting. We wondered if we would witness a coup.

I decided very quickly that I liked "the city of good airs". With its wide avenues, its statues, its plazas and cafes it was easy to see why it has been described as "the Paris of South America". It was a pleasant city in which to stroll: it seemed easy to escape the traffic on either the wide pavements or the many pedestrianised areas. We took a stroll at around 10.30 pm and the streets were thronging. The street in which we stayed had nothing but small hotels, restaurants, cafes, ice cream parlours, cinemas and the occasional Exchange House or Cambio. We could not help but be struck by how smart and smartly dressed the people all were. Was this country really suffering an economic crisis?

It was. On our arrival into Buenos Aires we had received 1,900 Argentinian Australes for one American dollar. Four days later a dollar was worth nearly 3,000 Australes. The Argentinian currency was becoming worthless. It was not only foreigners who were queuing at the Cambios every day, the locals were doing it too. They could not afford to keep any unnecessary Australes and would trade them in for dollars keeping only sufficient for perhaps their next meal or two. The Argentinian who did not do so could find himself only half as well off at the end of the week as one who did.

It is all too easy when travelling on the cheap to let the challenge of getting the best deals and living on almost nothing take over, distracting and detracting from the task and hopefully the pleasure of seeing and experiencing new countries. Amongst young travellers, conversation generally revolves around money: tips on the cheapest hostel here, the best exchange rate there and a free meal somewhere else . . . it seems to be an obsession and it had turned us, and Jo in particular, somewhat anti travellers.

In Buenos Aires, although we did not see many travellers, we did find ourselves devoting some energies and thoughts to obtaining the best exchange rate, or perhaps I should say I did, because Jo still seemed to think it was a lot of fuss about a few pennies (which admittedly it was). The fact remains that if you had a meal and then left to convert your dollars in Australes it was a cheaper meal than if you had already changed them. So Jo would remain seated trying to hide her embarrassment whilst I hurried around the nearby Cambios for the best rate. It reminded me of history lessons at school when we were taught about inflation under the Weimar Republic in Germany between the Wars: "They had to pay for their coffee before drinking it," our teacher had explained, "because afterwards it would be dearer". Imagine that, I had thought then; I no longer needed to – it was happening all around me.

It was not however so much the increase in prices, which were perhaps made daily or even weekly (the latter could exceed 100%) that caused the near permanent queues at the Cambios; it was the constant decline of the Austral against the dollar, often by several percentage points whilst you waited in the queue.

"How can the people look so smart and the restaurants be so busy when the currency is in such decline?" we asked a local. "It's a question of pride," we were told, "Argentinian people are very proud; they love to look smart, to dress up and go out for dinner. They put all their money into it; they may live in cramped and crumbling accommodation but they have to look as if they are doing well. Appearances are everything."

Our week in Buenos Aires was one in which we could hardly claim to have stretched ourselves. It was partly because, after weeks of apparently stifling heat, the clouds had opened and we had experienced almost non stop rain. So there was an excuse, and we certainly seized it. Days were spent alternating between cinemas, cafes, ice cream parlours and restaurants and of course the inevitable visits to the Cambio. We knew we would not be in a city for some time (it turned out to be seven weeks) and enjoyed the gluttony and over indulgence whilst we could.

Talk of Buenos Aires cannot possibly end without a mention of one of its most famous products; its steaks. In these days of cholesterol counting and vegetarianism it is perhaps no longer quite the done thing to eat large steaks for lunch and supper. Neither Jo nor I are big meat eaters but our succulent rump or fillet steaks as tender as a turnip, and salads, with a bottle of marvellous Argentinian red wine served by immaculately dressed and discerning waiters was a definite highlight of Argentina, if not the trip as a whole. If we could enjoy a meal of such quality in England I would be interested to know where, and would expect little change from £50. It made not one iota of difference to our enjoyment of it that there was plenty of change from a fiver; it merely meant that even budget travellers like ourselves living on £16 a day for both of us could enjoy what at home would be considered a rare treat.

Chapter 7

WE TOOK A NIGHT TRAIN south to Bahia Blanca. The scenery was flat and farmed, yellowy green, virtually treeless, not terribly exciting and reminded me of parts of North Humberside. We sat on a brown plastic three person bench and the train was packed; it seemed that a lot of people would be standing throughout the night. A man clad in a white shirt, black bow tie, velvet jacket and black trousers, resembling something between a 1930's Noel Coward and a1990's John Parrot, appeared with a tray of beer, soft drinks, sandwiches and coffee.

It was a shame that the same attention to appearance and to passenger comforts did not extend to the train's lavatories. They comprised four bare walls and a hole in the floor. There was no sink, water, chain or loo paper, there was a lot of dirt and I do not even want to say what else; suffice to say you had to take a deep breath before entering and could not release it until some distance away. We fell asleep to the sounds of country and western music and a crying baby.

Bahia Blanca was, and I have no doubt still is, a boring city. The *South American Handbook*, our (and indeed many other South American travellers') Bible says of Bahia Blanca: "It has some fine modern buildings, two parks and a very poor zoological garden". Considering it has a population of 300,000, that is hardly much of an accolade.

Why, you may be wondering, did we choose to go there. It is quite simply that Bahia Blanca is the best placed city from which to enter Patagonia, the vast desert at the bottom of the world. It is a desert which covers more than one quarter of Argentina's land mass and is several times the size of England. The population, 600,000, can only be described as staggeringly low.

28

Patagonia has been referred to as "the Uttermost part of the earth" and as one of the least likely regions of the world to suffer from attack. Our appetites had been whetted by reading *In Patagonia*, an account of the late Bruce Chatwin's wanders in the early 1970's and more particularly of the variety of people whom he met. We were under no illusions about the scenery: it would in the main be flat, treeless and very very dull.

Since the attraction was supposedly the people, and since distances were vast and our Australes running low, we decided to chance our arm at hitch hiking.

"Take a short bus trip to the service station on the main road," the locals advised us, "there will be plenty of traffic going south."

We did but there wasn't. Three hours later we hadn't moved an inch. This had all the makings of a disaster: you had to travel so many hundreds of miles to reach anywhere of note that we even contemplated the awful prospect of returning to Bahia Blanca and trying for a bus. Thankfully this horrendous thought was swept aside when a lorry stopped for us.

The driver was bearded, in his forties, several stone overweight, all of it sagging over his belt, and his eyes, though sad, were friendly and genuine. He did not speak a word of English. The passenger was slightly built and slightly Chinese looking, possessed of a cheerful disposition and near permanent smile, and, despite telling us that he had learnt English for five years, appeared to know only a handful of words. They were heading for Neuquen, some 400 miles west of Bahia Blanca, which was a good distance for us to go but for the fact that it was in the wrong direction.

After 100 miles or so of flat countryside of straw coloured grass devoid of trees, buildings and people, and of virtually dead straight road almost devoid of traffic, the option of being dropped in the middle of nowhere for a lift south, which would have to be for hundreds of miles to reach anywhere, was one which it did not take us long to dismiss. We would go to Neuquen.

Our driver was baffled by our desire to visit Patagonia and seemed visibly shaken when we told him of our plans to spend several weeks there. "Hey nada en Patagonia" he kept repeating ("there is nothing in Patagonia") remonstrating with his hands and on one occasion banging his fist on the steering wheel and on another turning towards us and veering off the road into the desert. It was a little disconcerting to see how upset he seemed, not to mention wondering if we really would be spending weeks in an area where there was nothing. "Nada Nada" he repeated. His friend just smiled but since he did so all the time anyway this was no aid to his feelings either on the area or on his friend's agitated state.

Looking back, I think I can now understand our driver's attitude. Could it perhaps be compared to giving a lift to foreigners travelling in England and learning that they will spend a great proportion of their time exploring Doncaster? Those who love England may perhaps feel angry and upset that our visitors appear, with as much respect as it is possible to give to Doncaster, to be missing out on a lot else. His anger and upset were, I suspect, the result of a passionate patriotism and pride which Argentinians possess in no small measure, combined with the intense boredom derived from having to drive a lorry so frequently through his country's harshest and least exciting scenery.

Fortunately shortly after our driver had veered off the road, we managed to veer him off the subject. We were soon back in trouble again. Somehow the discussion got round to the Falklands. There was more banging of fists on the steering wheel. Our driver's excitement rose to such fever pitch that his words became quite incomprehensible and we took the easy way out, nodded agreement and changed the subject. The passenger just kept on smiling.

The scenery continued to be flat, desolate and treeless. It was a desert of small shrubs rather than a sand desert, reminiscent of the Nullabor Plains in Western Australia.

After some six hours the scenery suddenly came to life and the last hour or so into Neuquen could almost be described as interesting. There were vineyards and orchards of apple, pear and peach trees, and poplar trees to shield the orchards from the sun. It became greener and even a little hilly although they were very low lying. We saw a few sheep but, despite endless signs warning of them crossing the road, not a single cow on the entire journey.

Neuquen, populated by some 60,000 people, had the look of a modern developing city. Many high rises were being built, a feature normally anathema to both Jo and to me, and yet we both had a good feeling about Neuquen. It was very clean and the people seemed both busy and friendly at the same time, not always an easy combination.

Located several hundred miles from any town of significance, Neuquen's principal purpose is to serve the orchards to the east (a lot of farm machinery is manufactured there) and the oil fields to the west. So it is in essence an industrial town but it also has to provide for the basic needs of people from a large radius. For somewhere so isolated it had a wide range of well-stocked shops which certainly gave more of an impression of prosperity than of a bankrupt country in turmoil.

We could not help but be struck by how happy the people seemed. It must be the sense of community spirit, of belonging and of seeing your own town progressing from within, we decided. There was no evidence of class barriers, we saw no beggars and no real signs of poverty nor of great wealth.

Looking back, I have to confess to wondering how we could have analysed what can at best really only be described as a very ordinary town in such depth and even more come to conclusions about it, based on one evening there and what Jo had gleaned from a discussion with the local who cut her hair. If a Neuquen expert is by any chance reading this and considers it a lot of claptrap, please bear in mind the rather limited basis on which our thoughts were formed.

Chapter 8

WE WERE BACK "ON THE ROAD" again the next morning. As in Bahia Blanca, the locals had advised us to take the bus to the main road south. "There will be lots of lorries," they assured us. There were not. Finally, after nearly three hours on the roadside, one pulled over for us, or rather for Jo, as I had gone on an information seeking wander. This may have been fortunate, not for the information which I gathered but because I suspect that Jo was the main attraction. "Not that old chestnut," he must have thought when she informed him her boyfriend was waiting in the wings somewhere.

It was a relief to be progressing. Our driver, who spoke no English, was considerably slimmer and softer spoken than the one of the previous day although in neither of those two categories would it have been difficult to be. He was going half way to what we had now decided was our temporary final destination, the Swiss style skiing resort of Bariloche in the Argentinian Lake District. He would drop us about 150 miles short of it. Things were looking up: we should arrive there tonight.

Sadly the route was horribly boring; low shrubs again, more sandy than yesterday, devoid of trees and painfully flat. It was like a drive up the A11 without the interesting bits. What made it worse was that the lorry appeared to have a maximum speed of about 30mph. Was it too much to ask just for a slight gradient, even a low lying hill in the distance, a tree, a building, a turn in the road or even a turn of speed? Unfortunately it was. Even the sight of another vehicle was a temporary reprieve from the monotony but occurred only about once every half an hour. At one point our driver informed us that we were approaching a big hill. He changed gears and slowed down in preparation and a worried expression came over his hitherto cheerful face.

"I have to be careful," he told us to our great pleasure and relief, "The road suddenly goes downhill."

We eagerly awaited it and looked ahead, no sign of it yet and the road as ever was dead straight. He really is being extremely cautious, we thought. And then he lit a cigarette and smiled and relaxed. "How far away is it?" we asked, a little perplexed.

"What?"

"The hill."

"That was it," he replied, equally perplexed. We looked back: it was just possible to make out a slight and very gradual slope in the road.

After two hours of nothing we had just experienced the most exciting part of the journey without even knowing it. What was worse, there were still three hours to go.

Thankfully it did improve. Dare I say it even became a little hilly in parts. There was wire netting to keep the animals off the road and signs telling drivers to "watch out for animals". There were however no animals.

The whole journey, apart from a few horses towards the end, was as free of animals as it was of everything else. At one point our driver told us we were approaching an estancia. This again got us quite excited. He said it is called "Hotel Ranch" and is owned by an Englishman. We crawled on several more painful miles.

"Where is the estancia?" we asked eventually.

"Here," he replied.

We looked in all directions but saw only the same boring flat fields as ever. He must have detected our confusion. "It is very very big." he informed us. It must have been: we were apparently driving alongside it for half an hour or so and could see for miles in any direction and never saw a building.

"What type of farming is it?" we asked.

"Animals."

We should have known. Needless to say we never saw any.

He dropped us off in Piedra del Aguila which literally means "stone of the water". It was the first "town" we had reached since leaving Neuquen five hours earlier. The word "town" is misleading:

it had one main street and only a few others and catered largely for truck drivers. It was 7.30 pm and we were starving. A quick bite and carry on hitching, we thought, only 150 miles to go. The service station didn't do meals, but recommended the restaurant over the road; they weren't serving for another hour but suggested another. "At this time!" the man in the next one exclaimed, laughing, "it's only 7.40."

"Perhaps we should go on," Jo suggested very sensibly but by now I was close to collapse cursing their ridiculous hours and could think of nothing but having a meal.

A little family run shop saved the day; they could do a pizza for us. It was quick and vast – just the ticket – and we chatted to the family who could not have been friendlier. Nourished again, what was really a fairly serious situation began to feel as it should: all part of the experience of travel. In the most unlikely of places where tourists never tread you can meet the most wonderful people and see their country in a different light.

"It is better to hitch later. You can catch the trucks driving through the night," we were advised. Locals' advice had not proved 100% accurate to date so we started earlier. Vehicles were few and far between: I would check out the hotels whilst Jo would chance her thumb. All three hotels were full; as I came back Jo was in conversation with a policeman. I feared the worst, thinking that maybe hitch hiking is illegal, and approached with trepidation. I need not have worried: he was suggesting to Jo that if we got stuck there may be a cell in the police station for us. It sounded desperate but after another hour or two without a lift so were we.

It was 10.00 pm and although still light we decided we had had enough. The police station was tiny and appeared to be staffed by one man.

"I am sorry," he said with genuine sympathy, "I have just got a prisoner in and we are already putting another couple up in the other cell."

It was obviously not unusual for the police station to double up as a sort of hotel when places were scarce elsewhere. He was clearly not going to leave us to roam the streets and made phone calls to the local hospital and a few friends until one of the latter said he could put us up.

A fellow police officer, he was round in a flash and on the five minute walk kept apologising that his house was very small. On opening the front door we were immediately into the main room – a room comprising bare walls, a stone floor and endless children. It seemed rather damp. "We had a very heavy rain recently. It came this high," our new found friend explained, holding his hand a foot or so above the floor.

He gradually introduced us to the children. When he called one his wife, we had thought our Spanish was the problem – she did not look old enough. It transpired that she was fourteen but yes, she was his wife and what is more she was pregnant. The others were all his wife's brothers and sisters.

Later a much older lady arrived. "My mother-in-law," our friend explained, "she has a hard life. She has twelve children." Biscuits and cakes were quickly produced to be equally speedily devoured by the mother-in-law who, until we saw how much she ate, looked as if she might have had a thirteenth on the way. They were accompanied by the inevitable mate, a drink which our truck driver had offered us and which appears to be every bit a part of Patagonian life as tea is in England. It comprises very sour herbs which are spooned out of a sachet and placed into one end of an instrument called a gourd which resembles a pipe. You then add a lot of sugar (or at least they do) and boiled water and suck the flavour in from the other end of the gourd. It is supposed to be very health giving which I expect it is if you keep it to yourself. There was however a social ritual of passing the gourd on; suspecting that the gourd may not be all that would be passed on if we participated, we had to tell them that we did not like mate which gave some offence but not as much as the real reason would have done.

Conversation was rather bitty. We showed them some postcards of England which got them very excited and we mentioned the Falklands which meant nothing at all to them. They produced a world map and we pointed out the Falklands. They gave a knowing smile, "Ah, Las Malvinas." Our friend the police officer then explained that he could not understand why the Argentine government wanted Las Malvinas. "It was obvious your government would defend. They had to defend."

The family showed us remarkable kindness and insisted on giving us one of the two bedrooms which left about eight of them crammed into the other. Just before bed we were introduced to yet another member of the family; the parrot.

We fell asleep that night to the parrot's piercing squawks surrounded by posters of Sting, Maradona and Rambo and thinking what an uncanny habit travel has of producing something out of nothing.

Chapter 9

JO AND I SPENT what could by no stretch of the imagination be considered a romantic Valentines Day morning trying in vain to hitch hike out of Piedra del Aguila. It was 2.15 pm before we succeeded. Again I can take no credit. I had remained on the roadside whilst Jo tried her luck in the service station and soon emerged with a triumphant smile on her face. She could not have done better than Jorges. He spoke some English, perhaps on a level with our Spanish, was in love with Bariloche where he used to live, and, the height of luxury, had a car. No more cramming into the front of a lorry and going 30 miles per hour. Our happiness was complete almost immediately after setting off and discovering not only hills but windy roads as well. After a short while we even saw snow capped mountains in the distance. How much more inspired we felt being whisked along in comfort through varied landscape.

Jorges was in his mid thirties, tall, dark, slim and moustachioed, classically Argentinian. A customs officer, he had spent many years in his beloved Bariloche but six years ago was moved to Buenos Aires which he found much less friendly. He loved the mountains and the lakes around Bariloche, the feeling of freedom and the people. We could see him becoming more and more excited as his old home loomed. He had driven all the way from Buenos Aires: 20 hours or so for a journey which had taken us four days.

Suddenly, we saw a most wonderful sight: as we reached the Nahuel Huapi Lake, Jorges pointed to a cluster of low buildings nestled in the lowest part of the hills on the other side of the lake still many miles away. "That," he said with evident and justifiable pride, "is Bariloche." Now we knew why we had come all this way: the view alone would refresh even the weariest of travellers. We could not wait to reach it; the thought of being on the edge of a

37

vast expanse of water and of having shops and restaurants (in short civilisation), on our doorstep after what had seemed like an eternity in the desert was almost too much. We felt a resurgence of energy. And I thought (and I hope Jo did as well) that it may be a romantic Valentines Day after all.

Jorges dropped us at the home of a lady who had little chalets for rent. We felt sad to leave the man we now referred to as "Jorges our Saviour" but he said he would see us the next day and there was no doubt that he was a man to keep his word.

Our temporary landlady was a lively lady in her late sixties who bombarded us with information as soon as we walked through the door but in a most pleasant and interesting way. She was a Yugoslav who had ended up in Austria during the Second World War and at the end of it found that Argentina was the only country which would take her. She had been here ever since.

"This country is in a terrible economic crisis," she told us sadly with an air of resignation, "we have good resources here, we should be doing well but there is so much corruption. This inflation is crippling. In December I lost two thirds of the rent because I took it in Australes. Now I have to charge US dollars."

For our double room with private bathroom we were charged six dollars a night. She was a proud and intelligent lady who did not deserve to be worrying about things like the price of milk and yet she did. Her husband's pension, paid in Australes, now amounted to 30 US dollars a month. In July and August she had had only two guests for four days. The Argentinians could not afford to travel, especially to somewhere considered as exclusive and expensive as Bariloche. "It can get very cold here in winter," she continued, "I am very worried. People will be hungry and cold. It's terrible."

Despite the obvious struggle to live from day to day which at times – and this was awful to see – reduced her almost to tears, she kept her standards and her interest in others and particularly in Bariloche which, despite her present troubles, she clearly adored.

"Bariloche is really a Swiss style town. You can see it in the wooden chalets and all the chocolate shops. But in fact it was founded at the end of the last century by two American brothers. Their grandchildren now run an estancia on the other side of the lake. It was actually an Italian who started the chocolate business. He became very wealthy but he never paid any tax. One day the tax inspector came to see him and he had a heart attack and died. It was such a shame because they worked out that he didn't have to pay much anyway."

I went out for a wander and found myself very quickly drawn to the water's edge. I just sat there staring across the vast lake, some 60 miles long and 8 miles wide and 460 metres deep in places, with the mountains around it. Water has always had a magnetic attraction to me, something about the sense of freedom and of space, of permanence and timelessness. I was oblivious to everything.

Everything, but not everyone. One person was as ever very much on my mind: Jo. We had been travelling together for six weeks, over a quarter of the total, and already I had a terrible sense of time slipping by, coupled thankfully with the desire to make the most of what we had. It was easy to take for granted her ability to put up with what really were often primitive and harsh conditions and still come out smiling. Tonight at least would be different. We found a lovely little wooden beamed restaurant, busy yet peaceful and relaxed, and enjoyed a delicious fondue and yet another excellent Argentinian red wine and I gave her some Swiss chocolates . . . a perfect evening from which even my getting us horribly lost on the way back to the chalet did not entirely detract.

True to his word Jorges arrived the next evening. "We're going to a friend of mine's house," he said, "he does the best barbecued steak in Bariloche." Frederico was a huge man who reminded me of the late Roy Kinnear. Bald apart from a few strands swept back on the top of his head and a hair line which started at the back of it, he had narrow glasses strapped round his neck which generally rested on his chest. He greeted us in English but only briefly allowed himself any distraction from the task in hand; it was clear that he treated the barbecueing of steaks with the utmost seriousness.

He and his wife had planned and built their house themselves over a period of several years. It was constructed largely out of pine and the pillars inside were quite literally tree trunks. The ceilings were high and beamed. There was a large brick fireplace, rifles and a deer's head (shot by a friend) on the walls, and the paintings were largely of horses. Town and County magazines lay on the table.

We enjoyed cooked cheese and oregano, empanadas (a popular Argentine snack of meat filled pastry like a miniature Cornish pasty) and Frederico's wonderful juicy fillet and T bone steaks washed down with bottles of San Juan, San Rocca, and San Felipe to name a few.

Their two daughters and their Chilean son-in-law were also there. The conversation was, for our benefit, in English; it was slow and measured which was I think fortunate for Jorges. We were interested to know when they had come here.

"That is a long story," Frederico began. "I originate from Holland. But I was only four years old when I came to Argentina. My father was an editor of a Dutch newspaper and he was warning the people there about the threat of Hitler. He had foreseen what would happen but not many people had. He became very unpopular and had to leave the country. Argentina was a long way away. It was better for my father to be out of Europe."

He had been in Argentina ever since in various parts. "My wife was brought up in Argentina too although her roots were a mixture of Italian and German."

"The interesting thing about this country," Frederico continued, "is that people come from all over the world. You know I was at a drinks party, there were perhaps 15 people there and we all came from a different country."

Briefly the conversation veered on to the Falklands. "Ah," Frederico sighed, smiling slightly and leaning back on his chair. "I have a different name for it." His alteration was to the second and third letters. "You know that was Galtieri's last stand. He had hoped to regain some popularity. It was not for Argentina he did it, it was for himself. Of course the British had to defend it: you cannot just let someone walk in and take over your people."

Towards the end of the evening the conversation switched to Spanish: they were discussing whether Argentina would be better with the Military again, I think concluding that it would not.

They spoke thoughtfully, one at time and slowly, although not quite slowly enough for me to understand a lot and for Jo to understand everything. How much we would have loved to have participated as they had done in our language. "How is it," we asked, "that you all speak such good English?"

"We learn it in the schools. After a certain time in each day the children are only allowed to speak English. Plus we read English magazines and books. Most educated people in Argentina will speak good English." There must be a lesson there.

We had a very active next few days; walking and climbing, playing tennis with Jorges, swimming in the lake and visiting a few of its islands (by boat rather than by swimming I have to confess). Bariloche was a perfect place to restore energy. The air was fresh, the climate warm, the views breathtaking and restaurants many and varied. Sadly we were several months too early for the skiing season.

Some 15 miles south of Bariloche along the lake, past some lovely brick and wooden houses with long gardens reaching down to the lake side, we saw an exceptional building standing on the top of a hill in its own grounds.

"It's a hotel called the Llaollao," (pronounced Chaochao) a fellow walker informed us, "but it's closed. It's been closed for 13 years. The Government owns it but it can't find anyone to buy it. The Club Mediterranean looked at it but thought it would cost too much to renovate and the economy is so unsure it's just too risky."

So this hotel, with a view overlooking a lake in open country with good walking and swimming, even a sandy beach on its doorstep, and with easily sufficient land for swimming pool, tennis courts and probably whatever other facilities it wanted, and seemingly with potential for 50 or more rooms, lay dormant. It was a sad symbol of its country: a country whose resources had made it one of the 10 richest nations in the world only 60 years ago and yet now those same resources, both the land and the people, appear to be going to waste.

It is hard to find an explanation. Clearly the political instability and regular military coups and the crisis in the economy are big factors. Yet it appears to me that they are a result of a deeper problem which even some Argentinians, despite their nationalistic feelings, were prepared to admit, namely their inability to work together as a team. That very feature which made it such an interesting country for us and which should give it a richness and a diversity was perhaps its greatest problem and ultimately its downfall.

"There is really no such thing as an Argentinian," I recall one explaining to us, "we are Russians and Poles, Welsh and English,

Swiss and Italians, Jews and Arabs. We are everything. The Jews came here because it was safe after the war and so did the Nazis. Is it any wonder we cannot get along with each other?"

Tennis with Jorges "our Saviour" and his girlfriend.

Chapter 10

FROM BARILOCHE we decided to head down south. We had read and heard about the Welsh living in Patagonia and were interested to see the towns in which they had settled. Two such towns were some 150 miles south. "The road is terrible. It will take you days," we had been told. It was hard to believe. Or at least it was until we saw the road. Then we wondered if we would ever make it. Hitch hiking, we were advised, was out of the question – there is simply no traffic. This turned out to be sound advice too, so we sat on a bus for four and a half hours as it bumped along a stony dusty dirt track at perhaps an average of 20 mph. I cannot even recall whether we ever saw another vehicle and certainly there were no towns or even villages, just one solitary cafe where we took a much needed break from being catapulted up and down.

Finally we reached El Bolson, some 60 miles short of the Welsh towns. In Spanish this means "The Bag". The town is surrounded by mountains, those to the west being the Andes.

Frederico had a sister who lived there, by the name of Poppy, and she in turn had an American girl staying temporarily with her called Barbara. Barbara met us at the bus station in a truck and transported us a short way into the mountains to Poppy's house. Poppy herself was confined to bed with a broken ankle but was clearly the sort of person whose zest for life was too much to let a little thing like that affect her.

"El Bolson," she informed us, "is the centre of the Argentinian hippy community. Basically anything goes. There are marijuana plants all over the place. It's so isolated here – hours from anywhere – its like a little world of its own." It seemed however to be a world that Poppy loved. And Barbara loved it too – she had come here to complete a thesis in tranquil surroundings and we had to think she could not have chosen much better.

For us, El Bolson was a classic example of a place made by the people you meet. Were it not for Frederico and then Poppy and then Barbara we may have stopped a night to rest, thought it seemed a lovely setting but otherwise nothing special, and headed off the next morning. But Barbara's enthusiasm was quite infectious: "You've got to see the hippy market. Oh and wouldn't you be fascinated to meet some of the Welsh here, descendents of the original immigrants. And did you know you can climb the Cerro Lindo and get to the top of the Andes." To which our replies were yes, yes and no but we'd like to.

The hippy market took place every Thursday and Saturday and was clearly El Bolson's big event. Unlike many so called hippy markets there were actually several hippies at this one. There were stands selling home made jams, organic fruit and vegetables, T shirts, mate pots and alpaca to name but a few. We stopped at a waffle stand run by a Danish man who had bought 4,000 acres of land for £20,000.00 and lived off that and selling waffles two mornings a week. "Very few people do much work here," Barbara had told us. Certainly the concept of a 9–5 did not yet seem to have filtered through to El Bolson.

We had an impression of a strange mix of people with rather glazed expressions who did what they wanted, didn't mind what anyone else did and did just enough work to tide over. Many of them were apparently drop outs from America, rebels against the materialism and pressure of their own country. They could hardly have chosen a less materialistic or less pressured environment in which to get away from it all.

We began our ascent of the Andes rather later than we should have done one afternoon. "It's safer with a guide," the young girl in the Tourist Office had told us, "but you don't have to have one – it's arrowed all the way. It will be perhaps four hours to a little hut where you can stay the night then a few hours more to the top." We decided our budget did not stretch to the luxury of a guide although it would only have been around a fiver from memory, and off we set, Andes bound, with just some spare clothes, not much food and cameras.

The first hour was extremely easy and only took us to the foot of the mountain. We reached a narrow stretch of water – perhaps only 30 feet wide but so fast moving that with cameras and my sense of balance it wasn't worth chancing. A scout or even someone with a modicum of practical sense would have sussed this one out in minutes. Not having been a scout or having even a modicum of practical sense, I stood there non-plussed.

Fortunately Jo is rather more adept in such situations and in no time had wedged a lengthy log between stones and instructed me to step over on it. After what seemed an eternity – apparently it did to Jo as well – I was on the other side.

There was no time to relax. A far more onerous task had been set for me. I was now required to make the most important catch of my life as Jo hurled her highly expensive camera across the river in my general direction. It was a good throw. I now had no excuse. The pressure was on. At stake: not only the continuation of our climb up the Andes but probably of the relationship as well. Even at nine–all in the fifth game of a squash match I hadn't felt pressure like this. Memories of primary school goalkeeping and of my hero Peter "the Cat" Bonetti rushed into my mind. Position yourself, get behind it, clasp it into your stomach. It seemed to hang in the air. I crouched, body behind it, hands together . . . and then suddenly there it was. Yes, I had got it. The camera was safe to live another day and so was I.

Worse was to come. A far faster moving and much wider and deeper stretch of water was soon in front of us. It was about fifty metres across. "We will never do it," I said to Jo, "we will lose our balance and the cameras will be in." "We've got to get across. Otherwise we can't do the climb." This was certainly true; the idea of turning back was clearly one that had not entered into her thinking.

I took a few tentative, shaky steps, camera held aloft, but the water was soon up to my shorts and the current, coupled with the uneven stony surface, made a fall inevitable. I turned back. "It's hopeless." Jo did not agree. We carried on downstream and stopped and spotted another couple crossing towards our side. The water was much shallower, not even up to their knees, but they seemed to be moving like snails.

45

"It's not too bad here," they shouted to us and then when they finally reached us they explained that there had been heavy rain last night. "It had been a piece of cake when we came a few days ago." So that explained it; both the Tourist Office and Barbara had referred to a few little streams early on. – "no problem, perhaps take a change of shoes". We had thought that either they were seriously prone to understatement or we were seriously lost.

This next hurdle overcome, we quickly began to ascend quite steeply. There was no time to pause. Two hours had passed already; it would be dark in another three. Now and again there was a red arrow on a tree and we breathed a sigh of relief; every time there wasn't and the path went two ways we cursed at the Tourist Office and probably also a little at ourselves. Were we really so hard up as to leave ourselves at risk of coming to grief half way up the Andes without a guide? Surely our lives were worth a little more than £2.50 each? It didn't bear thinking about so we chose to curse the Tourist Office instead.

The track, such as it was, comprised mainly just mud, although sometimes rock. It was lined by lots of trees. From time to time we looked back for a stupendous view over and beyond El Bolson to the mountain range on the other side of it. Mostly we just looked forward and up not even looking left or right, too breathless to talk. It seemed to get steeper with every step. We went on for two hours or so without coming across another soul or even a natural resting point.

It was 8.00 pm and starting to get dark. There was no clue as to how far it still was to the hut. It also became suddenly very cold. The T shirt and shorts in which we had sweated a few hours before were now woefully inadequate. Jo was shivering terribly. We stopped frequently to find something else to wrap around her.

Then we suddenly heard voices. They were above us. A lady and two children appeared. We were to say the least just a little pleased to see them. "Is there a hut further on?" we asked hopefully. "Ah, yes you go about another hour to a waterfall then it's not too far after that." "Another hour!" Our hearts sank. Poor Jo was so cold – I have never seen anyone look that cold but she was determined. She had that look in her eye, her heart was set on it, nothing would stop her. Yet this was a blow – another hour, more even, of relentless uphill climbing as it became darker and colder by the minute.

Finally we reached the waterfall; still no sign of any hut. The arrows ran out; we cursed again and took a chance but it led to nowhere. We wondered if we would ever make it and whether we could survive a night in the open. We took a different route and, what relief, a red arrow appeared – our life line. Yet more climbing and then we saw it. A grey building, it must be it. Our pace quickened in expectation but no, it was just a wall.

Surely we must be nearly there, we would have given anything to be suddenly transported under a hot shower in a warm room and put in front of a table of soup and bread and stew and potatoes. What irony there was in all of this. Whilst millions felt trapped in the monotony of routine in their warm houses, under the shower, eating supper or putting their feet up in front of the telly dreaming of things like climbing up the Andes and knowing in their hearts they never would, there we were doing it and yet dreaming only of the luxury they took for granted and beginning to wonder if we would ever have it.

We reached some level ground for the first time for hours. This must be a good sign; we saw grass – even better. Then with an expression of joy mixed with relief and with achievement Jo proclaimed that she'd found it. And there it was: no more than a stone building with two rooms but it was like a palace to us. Three Argentinian lads greeted us. "You must be freezing. Have some soup." Piping hot cups of tomato soup were thrust into our hands and blankets wrapped around us. We sat on stools of tree trunks by a small wood fired stove and were surprised at the speed of our return to relative normality and of the thawing out process.

"Weren't you worried?" one of the Argentinians enquired.
"Oh, not really," we replied, lying.
"You know several people have lost their lives climbing around here. It gets so cold at night. People have died of the cold. Others have fallen in the dark. It's so easy to get lost." It was only then that we fully appreciated the extent not only of our luck but also of the reckless disregard which we had had for our own safety.

We sat down to a hearty meal of spaghetti bolognese and lots of home-made bread (it had to be home made, they only collected food every few weeks) and several bottles of Argentinian Red. It was just the ticket. We talked of the Argentine economy (as always) politics and the World Cup.

"The trouble with Argentina," one of them said, "is the Argentinians. They are too lazy, too arrogant, they don't want to work."

He said it as if he was not one. This was not uncommon. They had all ended up in this country but their country was where they had come from; they could criticise without having to feel any personal responsibility.

"You've got a good football team though," I piped in hopefully when they seemed to be falling into a deep depression about Argentina's decline.

"We did have but it's not a team. They can't play together. Half of them don't even play in this country. We will not win the World Cup."

We slept on the stone floor in borrowed sleeping bags surrounded by blankets. A roof over our head, a floor, full bellies and a stream to wash in felt like paradise. It was a good night's sleep.

Chapter 11

WE AWOKE at about 10.00 am the next day and enjoyed some home-made bread, hard-boiled eggs and home-made apple and strawberry jam whilst the two Argentine supervisors studied maps to show us the route to the top. One of them, Rafael, then said he would accompany us. Whilst this took away part of the challenge, I have to confess that it came as something of a relief. Rafael, in typically self-effacing manner, explained that it was better for him to come because if we didn't return (and there was surely a fair chance of that) he'd end up having to search for us.

"It should take about six hours," he informed us. I made an appalling start confronted by an almost vertical section of not terribly secure rocks. Rafael and Jo scrambled up in no time and waited patiently as I took one painstaking step after another. There was then thankfully a flatter spell where we could walk easily and converse. Rafael talked again of the risks of the mountain.

"Only a few nights ago two men failed to appear. I searched and searched and finally found them at about 10.00 pm. They were extremely relieved and I have to say extremely fortunate."

We wondered if Rafael himself had ever been in such a situation.

"Yes," he replied "I have been lost twice, once it was for two days. Nobody knew I had gone. I had only a sleeping bag and two chocolate bars. Luckily I knew which plants to eat to survive."

"What about the other time?" we enquired.

"Oh, that was only for a day."

Throughout the climb, which was thankfully much less steep than the day before, we had quite stupendous views of both the Andean mountain ranges and the mountains opposite beyond El Bolson. As the summit neared we could see well into Chile. On a very clear day, such is Chile's narrowness, you can apparently see the Pacific Ocean. We could not, but the seemingly endless succession of mountain ranges to the west must have stretched for 50 miles or so.

Surrounded by mountains as we were it soon became easy to take it all for granted and become even a little blase. The sight of a waterfall and periodically of small lakes clicked us back to attention. One lake was particularly striking because of its green water. "It is usually tri-coloured," Rafael explained, "blue, light blue and green. for some reason this year it is only green. Nobody seems to know why."

Some four hours after setting off from the shelter and after perhaps ten hours climbing in total, Rafael pointed to what was on this scale really no more than one of many bumps in one of the ranges of mountains. "You see that summit there," he said, "that is *the* summit." It seemed barely distinguishable from all the other bumps but it would now only take some 20 minutes or so to achieve our goal. We had a second wind, like when you snatch a game at squash that you thought had got away, and that final twenty minutes, steep though I am sure it was, felt devoid of pain and there we were: 2,000 metres up at the top of the Andes.

Less than three days earlier we had not even known it was possible, not all that long before we had not even known it was there and less than 24 hours earlier we had been on the verge of turning back thwarted by an excessively fast flowing river. It was strange to think that only the night before, freezing nearly to death and searching in darkness for a tiny hut amongst miles upon miles of mountains, we would have given anything for the usual comforts of home. Yet, standing there with Jo, the feeling surprisingly was not of any great achievement or even of relief but of how really it had not been all that difficult. This was clearly ridiculous but it reflects I think the aura that the Andes holds.

Learning about this vast mountain range stretching for several thousand miles up the western side of South America conjures up images of expeditions of experienced climbers training for months kitted out with special clothing and shoes, ropes, detailed maps, sleeping bags, tents and bags full of liquids, food and sucrose tablets. The reality was far removed from this: clad in T shirt, shorts and training shoes with only a bag of bread and cheese and apples after

Shaun and Jo on top of the Andes.

Shaun in Argentinian Lake District near Bariloche.

Nomadic family in Tierra del Fuego.

Perito Moreno Glacier.

"The Falklands are Argentinas."

Housing in Gaiman,
'Welsh' village in Argentina

Ushaia, Tierra del Fuego,
foot of Argentina.

Llao Llao – the Hotel nobody will buy.

René Griffiths and his guanacos on his farm near Cholila.

no forward planning or training, and previous experience limited to walks around the countryside of Bath, we could hardly have been more amateurish and clueless.

The view from the top was of blue grey mountain ranges like vast solid rolling hills with jagged edges. There was a warm sun, a gentle breeze and an eerie silence. I cannot remember that we spoke much. It was enough just to look, reflect and be lost in our own thoughts. There was a small pole to mark the summit and a jam jar in which previous climbers left messages on scrappy bits of paper. We added ours but I forget what it said.

"You know," Rafael commented, "this is the lowest part of the Andes. It is 2,000 metres high but when you go further north into Peru and Ecuador it becomes much higher. The highest part is about 7,000 metres."

It was not intended in any way to diminish our achievement and nor did it. He was, I think, merely ensuring that we did not leave under any misapprehension and it is for this same reason that I mention it. It was enough for us to have reached the summit of this particular section and it had been sufficiently tough and sufficiently potentially disastrous that I think we both knew that we could give any higher summit a miss and still return home contented.

The return to the hut was relaxed and easy. Rafael told us of the conflicts between Chile and Argentina over these mountains and indeed over Patagonia in general.

"Chile is so thin and full of so many little islands. They need more space for their people and it would give them more security against Argentina to have more of Patagonia but it was hard deciding exactly where the border should be. It was going to be divided so Chile had the land up to the rivers whose source is the Pacific, and Argentina had the land whose source is the Atlantic. But the Chileans realised that by altering the route of one river they would all come from the Atlantic. It was left to a British Court to decide and it decided that the mountain ranges themselves should be the border. The actual customs are not on the border but at the foot of the mountains."

We enjoyed an evening in the Refugio with spaghetti bolognese and red wine both in considerable quantity whilst our Argentinian hosts veered from enthusiasm about the mountains to depression about the state of their country.

The descent to El Bolson the next morning was anything but relaxed and easy. It is said that more accidents occur climbing down mountains than up them. Such was the steepness that it was extremely difficult to avoid running away with yourself: you had to turn rather like in skiing at the bottom of a descent and it was all you could do to keep your balance.

Jo's knee, which she had injured badly in a skiing accident a few years before, was playing up, not really surprisingly in view of the pressure which must have been on it, and so we resorted to a routine whereby she would hold on to my side and pull me back and we tried to fight the force of gravity. This seemed to work to some extent though what it was doing to my hips and knees did not bear thinking about. We must have done this for most of the four hours or so of the descent.

The rivers that had caused such trouble on the way were now much shallower and presented no serious obstacle and by lunch time we were back in El Bolson. It seemed inconceivable that we had left less than two days earlier.

Chapter 12

AFTER UNINTENTIONALLY FALLING ASLEEP for the whole afternoon we paid a visit that evening on Ronnie Gough to whom Barbara had introduced us. Ronnie lives on a farm a few miles out of El Bolson centre with his Argentinian wife and children. He is one of a dying breed of descendants from the Welsh adventurers who came out to remotest Patagonia during the second half of the 19th century to set up what has been called "a little Wales beyond Wales". It is a most unusual story.

It arose out of the general dissatisfaction the Welsh felt in the last century (and it seems that some still do) at interference from the English. They wanted to maintain their own language and traditions free from the control of their dominant neighbours. But where to go? It would have to be somewhere undeveloped and not previously or at least hardly inhabited. Patagonia, given that even today it has only 600,000 inhabitants in an area several times the size of England, seemed to fit the bill. Two of them sailed over in 1863. They met with Argentinian Ministers and sought a promise of land for the Welsh on the East coast. The Ministers were not impressed and turned them down.

Undeterred, in 1865 153 high spirited patriotic Welshmen, women and children embarked on a voyage of discovery to the unknown territory many thousands of miles away where they would set up a new life for themselves. They sailed from Liverpool on a ship called "The Mimosa". Some three months later "The Mimosa" reached the East coast of Patagonia at a place subsequently called Puerto Madryn after one of the two who had made the original fact finding mission. They then discovered that in their attempt to set up home they had been beaten by the Indians by a few thousand years.

This may have turned out to be a blessing in disguise, for the Indians showed them where the rivers were and generally made them feel at home.

Over time more Welsh arrived although the last significant immigration was as long ago as 1911. Some did not remain: most notably in 1899, when a great flood drowned the valley, many departed for Canada. Nonetheless the dream of a "Little Wales beyond Wales" is still being kept alive. The original immigrants had built Welsh-speaking schools and churches both in the East where they landed and alongside the Andes on the west side of Patagonia where we now were. The Westerners would provide wool to the Easterners in return for money and food.

Ronnie told us of his great grandfather, a man called Llwyd Aplwan, one of the founding fathers of the Welsh colony. He told us how he had lost his life in 1909 when shot in the heart by a known gangster who had been hoping to raid his safe for the proceeds of wool sales.

"There are still some well known and well established Welsh families around El Bolson but the generation above me are dying and some of the traditions and feeling are going too. The children now are learning Spanish in the schools: they often cannot speak Welsh. It is a big change in two generations."

We also learnt from Ronnie something which was rather revealing about the Falklands War. He was serving in the Argentinian Navy at the time and because of his fluency in English and the fact that that was the language of the Falklands he was sent over there when the Argentinians first arrived to explain to the local people what was happening. He had expected to be there only a few days and it appears to have come as a surprise to the Argentinian leaders that the British reaction was not quicker and more decisive.

He had felt that the original arrival and showing of the Argentinian flag was an attempt merely to persuade the British that they would have to take the discussions and the negotiations seriously and give to them a sense of greater urgency. It was a surprise to Ronnie to be asked to stay on, a fact he attributes to the opportunism of the Argentine generals.

Chapter 13

WE DECIDED to hitch hike to Esquel a town of Indian origin developed by the Welsh and situated some eighty miles south of El Bolson. It should not have been difficult, but traffic was sparse and after many hours we had progressed only about ten miles.

The silence was eerie. It was hot and hazy. We stood on the roadside surrounded by blue mountains, not a person or vehicle in sight. It was attractive enough scenery, we thought, but we would happily swap it for a bit of progress. Eventually a bus arrived and with some relief and only a little doubt as to whether we could afford it we hopped aboard. After half an hour or so the bus stopped for 10 minutes in Cholila.

We had read of Cholila as the old stomping ground of Butch Cassidy, the infamous outlaw and original anti mormon rebel from Utah and of his sidekick Harry Longbaugh, the Pennsylvanian German better known as the Sundance Kid.

A 19th and 20th century Robin Hood, Robert Parker, alias Butch Cassidy, came from a Lancastrian family but had been brought up in Utah where he developed a detestation of the cattle companies and banks whom he saw as exploiting the poor. His ventures into the world of criminal activity started relatively tamely with the theft of some cattle, progressed (if that is the word which it probably is not) to holding up banks, and culminated in his involvement in some murders. He had met the Sundance Kid in New York and they fled together to Argentina where they thought, correctly as it transpired, that they would be fairly well out of reach of the U.S. authorities.

For some years they lived in Cholila. It is a mystery what finally happened to them, their bodies never having been found. It was easy to see why Cholila was a safe haven for them: mountainous and remote it now had only one stony street with a few shacks. Our bus stopped outside one which turned out to be a bar.

The atmosphere in the bar was striking: it was certainly very basic, comparable to the English roadside snack bar so beloved of truck drivers if not Environmental Health Officers, yet, instead of bacon and eggs and mugs of tea, this one offered large glasses of lukewarm white wine, nuts and seemingly little else.

One man, stocky with a shock of dark curly hair, unshaven and even a little unkempt, was playing the guitar; three others, their checked shirts and goucho boots and hats giving away their identity, were singing along with him.

It was like a scene from a Western; how interesting, we thought it would be, to try and chat with these people, to see the lives they lead in this one-road town of shacks some way from anywhere.

Unfortunately they did not seem the sort of people you could slap on the back and buy a drink for and anyway the bus would be going in a few minutes. Suddenly the music stopped.

"Where are you from?" asked the guitarist in Spanish, "I speak English, Spanish, Welsh and French."

"England," we replied.

"Fine," he continued, this being the first English word we had heard him utter and one which he was to repeat ad nauseam (do we really use it that much?), "Why not stay here? Everybody passes through Cholila. Stay. I will show you everything."

We said we were interested in Butch Cassidy.

"Fine, I'll show you where he was living."

I was very tempted; Jo looked less so which was hardly surprising. We spoke discreetly, Jo expressing concern at their apparently drunken state. There was something about the guitarist that made me feel he could be trusted. Travel is often about grasping the nettle, seizing the unexpected chance: we grabbed our rucksacks from the bus and left ourselves to the mercy of these four strangers.

"Is there somewhere to stay?" we asked.

"You stay on my farm – a huge farm, lovely. Stay as long as you want."

I ordered a glass of wine for us. Jo was a little tentative and I thought it might help.

"Be careful with them," said the lady who served us. That was all we needed; now I was tentative too, but the bus had gone.

"How do you speak such good English?" we asked the guitarist. "I was in Wales 12 years, I was an actor."

As if to prove the point he then started singing Welsh songs with one of the others. "My brother," he explained although they could hardly have looked less similar. Tall, lean, ginger haired, hard faced and generally unapproachable, the brother was not a man we warmed to.

The other two seemed quiet and a little confused by us – one was Arab looking, well into his forties, the other young, chubby with a friendly face.

In between bouts of singing we had brief conversations with the guitarist during one of which he told us that his name is Rene. They all had several more glasses of wine and finished with a row with the landlady over the bill.

By now we were both fairly keen just to reach the farmhouse. Rene put us into the back of a pickup van and sat with us. The others remained in the bar, presumably still disputing the bill.

"My brother," Rene told us,"is a little crazy. He can get very drunk. Recently he put a revolver to my head."

At this, Jo, who had always been wary, turned a whiter shade of pale whilst I pretended both to her and to myself that this was all just part of the experience. I don't think it fooled Jo although I may at least have temporarily succeeded in fooling myself. Finally the others emerged and we headed off.

We had been going for about 30 minutes, the last 15 of them along a dirt track, and even I was beginning to wonder, when Rene suddenly proclaimed that we had arrived. This merely heightened our anxiety; it did not seem to us that there was anywhere to have arrived at. There was no gate, no sign or other identifiable landmark; we just carried on along the same dirt track with shrubs and thistles on either side.

Several more minutes passed and still no sign of anything. "I thought we'd arrived."
"We have, this is all mine. All my land." Rene exclaimed with evident pride, "I have 1,200 acres here."

Finally, after what seemed an eternity but was probably another 10 minutes, we stopped. There was a small caravan and two cars. We wondered where the farmhouse was.

"Where do you live?" we asked Rene.

"Here," he replied pointing to the caravan: it was tiny – two bunk beds, a cooker, table and chairs, it was certainly much smaller than many people's front room yet all four of them clearly lived there.

"It's OK," Rene continued obviously detecting our puzzled expressions, "You don't have to sleep in here." At this Jo relaxed visibly. "You can sleep wherever outside – or you can use one of the cars." Not exactly spoilt for choice but certainly preferable to the caravan.

We made a fire outside and sat by it chatting with Rene whilst the others prepared supper. Rene clearly enjoyed little more than to sit outside with a bottle of wine in the glow and warmth of a fire and reminisce about his travels. He had gone to Wales to see the country of his ancestors, had worked there and in Europe and only returned to his native country a year or so ago, after some seventeen years away, fired by an ambition to become a guanaco farmer. He was to tell us much more about guanacos later, but the wine, the fire and meeting fellow travellers had put him in a reflective mood.

He seemed a man who lived on his wits. He had hitch hiked widely, been deprived of everything by thieves in Colombia and went to Wales knowing not a word of English or Welsh. He both seemed and looked much younger than his 40 years.

We were called into the caravan for supper: with six of us crammed in, it was full to capacity. We had some noodle soup with bits of meat which was home-made and tasty. The other three all seemed very quiet; the brother looked less friendly even than before. He then picked up a meat knife and started waving it around. I looked at Jo; she was clearly petrified. I looked at Rene. He was reassuringly calm and was telling us in English not to worry. "It's just his little game."

The problem was that Rene was not saying anything to his brother. Or at least I thought at the time that that was the problem, but it may actually have been for the better. There was no point in trying anything on: we were not going to get out of that caravan

58

and even if we had there was nowhere to go. So there was, to say the least, an uneasy silence. The brother waved the knife in front of our faces and held it at Jo's throat. I tried to look suitably impressed and to compliment him in Spanish thinking that this may be a "I may not be able to speak English but I can do things with a meat knife you wouldn't even dream about" sort of threat.

Had he actually looked like using it on us I can only think that instinct would have brought us to react and try to grab it from him. I do not know how long all this lasted: no doubt it seemed much longer than it really was but it was several minutes at least. Each time he waved the knife at us he grinned, an inane grin: he really was a most unpleasant piece of work.

I was once again painfully aware of our vulnerability. Travel of the sort that we were doing, working it out ourselves as we were going along, inevitably involves taking risks. If this drunken gaucho decides to knife us to death and buries our bodies anywhere in this remote farmland who on earth will know about it? The lack of post may eventually alert people back home but a month could easily elapse before it did, and what could be done anyway? Nobody could know we were going to Cholila, we did not even known ourselves until arriving there.

All too frequently, I can hardly believe the dangers to which I have exposed myself. This time was far worse: I had exposed Jo to them as well. Every time, as when I became blindingly drunk, I tell myself it must never happen again; experience had unfortunately shown that, in both cases, sooner or later it will. Maybe one day I will be able to enjoy the comforts of life without feeling I have first to endure the discomforts.

Finally "the game" was over. The knife went back into the belt at the back of his trousers where, it only then dawned on us, it seemed that he always kept it. This had not exactly whetted our appetites and I cannot recall having anything more than a few bowls of soup.

In Italy the poor would fill you with pasta to depress your appetite for the main course and in Yorkshire they did, and indeed still do, it with Yorkshire Pudding, onion and gravy. The poor Argentinian gauchos' method of noodle soup blended with a smattering of knife waving was the most effective appetite suppressant I have yet to come across.

It was with some relief that we departed the caravan with Rene to return to our fire leaving the brother to the washing up. "My brother is generally OK," Rene assured us, "the problem is that he has to keep up a macho image. This is the gaucho image. I have worked on farms all over and it is always like this."

Having decided that the brother had now proved himself enough, or that there wasn't much we could do about it if he hadn't, we clambered into a Falcon, the bigger of the two cars there, for what proved to be something of a restless night.

Chapter 14

AFTER A COLD NIGHT we ventured out of the car as the sun was beginning to warm us and and as Rene appeared with some coffee and a bottle of white wine.

"Come with me," he said excitedly. He led us to his guanacos. What wonderful animals they were. A member of the camel family and much like llamas, Rene explained how he has collected about 70 of them from the Desert. "They are born in November and you have to get them quickly. Otherwise it can be hard to keep them tame." One, who had presumably been collected late, was kept tied to a post; the rest were free to roam.

They approached us: Rene clearly adored them and it seemed that the feeling was mutual. Their wool was thick and light brown, their heads perhaps five feet off the ground although the neck alone accounted for a least a foot of that. The sound they made was unforgettable: try keeping your mouth closed and saying "Mm" from the back of your throat and you will not be far off it.

"They are only a few months old, most of these," Rene informed us, "but you should see them move. They can go at 60 mph." Unfortunately we never did and it was hard to imagine but Rene certainly knew his guanacos.

We spent a fabulous day exploring Rene's farm, riding his horses and swimming in his lake. The lake itself must have been several square miles.

"This is the warmest water in the area," Rene explained, "strictly it is a lagoon rather than a lake because it is not from a glacier, so the water is warmer."

Returning to what could loosely be called "base", we saw one of the gauchos return with a recently killed sheep lying across the saddle of his horse. Rene explained that a knife had been inserted into its neck and it had died within seconds. The ribs and legs were removed and the ribs hung on a nail in the branch of a tree. The fire was prepared: an "asador" was placed in the ground at about sixty degrees from the fire and the ribs were then attached to it. The thin point could be turned cooking the lamb evenly. All this was done in concentrated silence.

Once ready, pieces of lamb were sliced off, dipped in a dressing, put on a chunk of bread and devoured with salad, washed down with white wine. The "asado" is a gaucho institution and I had rather assumed that it was also a great social occasion. Perhaps it is as a rule, but, if so, this one was certainly proving the exception. It may not of course have been wholly unrelated to our presence and to the incident of the previous night.

Rene's brother-in-law was also present and he was going to give both Rene and us a lift to our next destination, Esquel, where our bus had been going. By chance Rene had been planning to go to Esquel and, although it meant a tight squeeze in the back of a pickup already almost full of odds and ends and a motor bike, a bit of discomfort for a few hours was a small price to pay.

After a fairly flat and not terribly interesting journey, which apparently included passing a one and quarter million acre farm, we finally reached a hostel in Esquel at around 11.30 pm.

What an experience Rene had given us! We could barely take stock of it all. I think we felt some satisfaction in our original gamble, and certainly, although there were doubtful moments, it had been one we would never regret and never forget.

Yet I knew also that I felt happy to have left when we did: the harsh, macho environment of which I had also had limited experience in the Australian outback is not one with which I feel entirely at ease. Indeed, if anything, Jo was in the end keener to stay and bowed with some reluctance to pragmatism over her own gut feeling. It was a relief to me, I must confess, to have some privacy, a clean bed, hot shower and the knowledge that a town's facilities were but a short walk away.

Chapter 15

THE NEXT DAY was, through choice, a quiet one. I rose around mid morning, went out to change some money, had no drive to do anything else, and returned to bed.

In the afternoon we visited Rene's brother-in-law who was of Russian and Polish extraction and spoke reasonable English. Television news was showing pictures of floods in England, of elderly ladies being air lifted to safety, and of waterlogged villages, and then, yet more pictures of England, this time of Poll Tax rioters in combat with the Police. Our host looked rather more concerned for our safety than we felt.

"Looks very dangerous, your country," he commented, "is it safe to return there"?"

It seemed an extraordinary question knowing, or at least assuming as we did, that the pictures were of the worst extremes in both cases. Yet it was, from his point of view, quite under-standable. Do we not in England sit in the comfort of our homes and see pictures of fighting in Lebanon or Israel or read of drug barons in Colombia and coups in Panama and imagine how horrific and frightening it must be to live there?

The reaction we had received from people in England when informing them of this trip can, with a few exceptions, be divided into two. Those who had not been to South or Central America warned of the dangers and gave every impression that they wouldn't touch it with a barge pole: those who had, told us how beautiful it is, what a great time we will have and not to take any notice of people who have never been telling us how dangerous it is. It is easy to see how it is done, but to write off an entire continent as dangerous is clearly as absurd as South Americans seeing Poll Tax rioting and flooding in a few streets in England and deciding that a visit to Europe is too risky.

Later that afternoon we paid a visit on Ronnie Gough's aunt. She was not in, but her son arrived as we were standing at the doorstep. His first words were, "Do you speak English?" in English without a hint of surprise at two complete strangers on his doorstep.

He invited us in, and within a minute all three of us had a glass of Premium Whisky in our hands. He farmed Merino sheep. We wondered if he knew Rene.

"Ah yes, I think I know him. I met him at a week long farmers meeting. If I have the right man, he was a little drunk." We were able to confirm, based on that description, that he probably had.

His mother arrived shortly afterwards. She could easily have passed for a member of the English aristocracy.

"This country has been taken over by foreigners you know," she informed us just as a member of the English aristocracy might. "Even our President is an Arab."

We wondered if she knew Rene.

"I only met him once, it was in a pub, I seem to remember he was rather drunk."

By no stretch of the imagination can Esquel be described as an interesting or an attractive town. Like the much smaller town of Trevelin some 15 miles to the South, it had originally been an offshoot of the Welsh colony. Having first arrived in Patagonia in 1865, it was not until 20 years later that Welshmen crossed to the West to be alongside the Andes. The journey from Puerto Madryn, which can now be done comfortably by bus in about twelve hours, was for those pioneers a tough voyage by horseback or wagon which would take them between two and three months. It was to be another nine years, in 1894, before entire families were to undertake the trip.

Trevelin is still sufficiently small that its "Welshness" can to some extent be preserved. Indeed its history is very well documented in a wonderful Museum containing original photographs of those founding fathers and early settlers, and manned by their descendants. Esquel is much bigger, a modern and developed town whose Welshness has, on the surface anyway, all but disappeared and which seemed to me to lack buzz and character. It did however leave me with three main memories.

I well recall a meal in the Jockey Club which Jo and I enjoyed with Rene: simple but quite delicious, home-made vegetable soup, grilled chicken and lemon with vegetables and five bottles of excellent Argentinian red served impeccably by waiters in velvet jackets and black bow ties. It was a restaurant which you would go out of your way to visit in England even at five times the price, but sadly, such was the state of the Argentine economy, it was nearly empty. Despite this, the pride of the Argentinian would not allow the standard of service, presentation and taste to drop one iota from the very best.

Secondly I recall spending an entire morning searching for a bank which had any Argentinian currency. I came to think of Esquel as the town with no money. This may have been unfair: such was the decline of the Argentinian Australe that at that time there may well have been many other towns suffering the same plight.

My final memory is of two frustrating days, the first trying in vain to hitch hike out of Esquel to the east, and the second waiting a whole day for the night bus east. The second day was spent mainly in a cafe writing our diaries and post cards and letters home to the almost permanent sounds of Karen Carpenter's *You Needed Me*. Whether the owner was obsessed with the song or whether the record had got stuck we never found out but even by lunchtime we knew the words backwards and the bus didn't leave until half past eight.

In Trevelin, we enjoyed a traditional Welsh tea in a tea house run by a lady who, despite having never set foot in the land of her ancestors, nevertheless spoke Spanish with a bit of a Welsh accent and had her walls adorned with Welsh tea towels. We came across several similar tea houses and, although I have never been to one in Wales, it would not surprise me if the tea in a little village in the Patagonian desert is closer to the traditional Welsh tea than that which would be served by many in Wales itself.

Chapter 16

THE JOURNEY ACROSS ARGENTINA was, to the extent that we were awake and could see during the night, generally flat, and interest was presented only by high rocks rising from the road side.

It ended for us at about 8 o'clock in the morning in Trelew, a town founded by the Welsh, only some 30 miles from Puerto Madryn where the "Mimosa" had landed. The name reflects the Indian – Welsh "cooperative" which brought it about, Tre being the Indian word for town and Lew being a reference to Lewis Jones, one of its founding fathers. It lies on the Chubut River to which no doubt the Indians had led the Welsh and it was this which had made it an obvious location for development.

Trelew had the air of a pleasant and prosperous town, if not unduly exciting or beautiful. The legacy of the Welsh which was not otherwise obviously in evidence was commemorated in a museum in the old railway station. The same sad fate appears to have afflicted the railways as in England and the station, along with many others, had been closed in 1971.

After a few hours sleep we visited the Touring Club, described in the South American Handbook as the "social hub of Trelew" and as having the best coffee in town. Being rather partial both to social hubs and to good coffee, we strolled along. It did not disappoint.

The bar/cafe was a large, almost square room, with a high ceiling, cane chairs, dark and light blue tablecloths, an enormous number of bottles behind the bar, discreet yet attentive service and wonderful coffee. There was enough proximity to others to absorb the atmosphere of animated but relaxed conversation, and yet enough space between tables to feel private. It was a place at which no matter how you felt when you entered, you could hardly help but feel immediately relaxed and rejuvenated. Certainly it was the perfect antidote to a night bus of broken sleep, and that journey quickly seemed days rather than hours ago.

We decided to have lunch there as well. This was perhaps the most important decision of that day and it was undoubtedly the right one. The restaurant had a colonial feel: a square room split by two large central pillars, salmon pink walls and with the same high ceiling and cane chairs as the bar/cafe. We enjoyed white, fleshy salmon in vinaigrette, a soup of Vermicelli in a lamb stock, chicken and salad and finally fruit salad, disappointingly from a shop tin, to the sounds of Tom Jones.

After the rest of that day and night in Trelew, we felt ready to move on, and took the one hour bus ride to Puerto Madryn. It was a rather uninspiring route and sadly it transpired that this was to be a prelude to the town itself. It was pleasant to be on the coast again (Montevideo was the last time we had been, five weeks before) but the beach was stony and not terribly inviting, the buildings modern and it had the feel of a very ordinary town.

An attraction of Puerto Madryn, however, is the excursions which go from the town into Peninsula Valdez. We took one. The Peninsula itself is flat, the ground seemingly dominated by thorns, and for its landscape alone it was not really worth visiting. The attraction is its wildlife. We saw Flamingoes, Penguins, Sea Elephants, Sea Lions and Seals but missed out on the Whales which apparently frequent the area.

It is hard to imagine a much more simplistic life than that enjoyed, or perhaps endured, by Sea Elephants. They are big and cumbersome looking, have no ears, make no noise, spend most of their time on their back occasionally managing a short crawl, spend from April to October in the water and from November to March on land, copulating and looking after their offspring. It may be that there are people who would envy them but they hardly struck me as the sort of animals with whom if they could talk you would wish to sit down and have a beer.

Sea Lions on the other hand seemed altogether more interesting. They are very much smaller but in contrast to the silence and inactivity emanating from the Sea Elephants they were full of action and seemed incapable of shutting up. The fathers "roared", mothers "mooed" and babies "baad". The roars were notably infrequent. Apparently the males copulate with up to thirty females and the poor babies often do not know who their father is. The one parent family syndrome is clearly not limited to humans.

The mothers, however, take the responsibility of parenthood seriously. It is a hard life; they have to look after the babies on land (the babies cannot swim for the first three months) but also have to go to sea to obtain food. What happens is that the babies are put in an equivalent of a creche and a few mothers look after them whilst the rest go to do the shopping. The community spirit which appears to exist amongst the mothers would no doubt be the envy of many a neighbourhood watch scheme or tupperware group.

Back at our hostel in Puerto Madryn that evening we met a tattooed Canadian lorry driver called Al. He asked us where we had been and where we were going, and before we had answered, told us where he had been and was going. He had apparently hitch hiked to Iran, managing to be attacked en route in Turkey, had found Colombia to be reasonably safe, and described Peru as an experience but not one which he would wish to repeat. His story of seeing two French travellers being shot dead by terrorists on a bus went some way to explaining why.

Later in the evening we heard three Germans discussing terms with the hostel owner for hiring a car to visit Peninsula Valdez. The Germans were clearly becoming animated, a state into which I have, with a few exceptions, only ever seen Germans get when discussing money, or more specifically the cheapest way to do something.

"Big Al", as we called him amongst ourselves, then intervened explaining to the Germans in English and at some length that the thing to do is to bargain for a low fixed sum and high mileage rate and then fiddle the meter. At this the Germans seemed somewhat dumbfounded but when they realised that it involved saving money even the thought of some rather unGermanic law breaking brought a smile to their normally placid faces.

They quizzed Big Al at some length in English, leaving the hostel owner waiting, not understanding a word, and then did the same in Spanish to the hostel owner leaving Big Al a little lost for words, a state which was clearly anathema to him.

It was difficult for us to believe that the Germans could firstly be so unaware of others and secondly be so pedantic and penny pinching. Their consideration of the cost of hiring a car must have lasted an hour, and the possible difference for a whole day's car hire came to a matter of a few pounds between them. It is that sort of attitude which can so easily give travellers a bad name amongst the locals and frankly the locals can hardly be blamed if they see travellers only in terms of money.

The next morning we were awoken at 7.00 am by some shouting. It was the Germans. Presumably it would not have been beyond them to approach each other and speak quietly, thus avoiding the necessity for everyone else to wake up, but, involving consideration of others as it did, it could not have been expected.

The morning continued in the frustrating way in which it had started. We needed some Australes for the bus back to Trelew, but no bank could give any.

"It's not possible," we were told in the usual Argentinian manner, devoid of sympathy and apology.

"Why not?," we enquired thinking that perhaps Esquel was not alone in having banks with no money.

"We don't have the exchange rate."

This was unbelievable.

"We have to wait for it from Buenos Aires."

Whilst the fax machine may not have reached the Argentinian provinces yet, the telephone certainly had and why they couldn't obtain the rate was quite beyond us.

"Come back at 11 we will be open for you then."

We did but they weren't. "Mas O Menos," we were told when querying this, a classic Argentinian phrase meaning "more or less" which seems to cover and excuse any eventuality. "More or less at 11" turned out to be 11.40 by which time we had missed several buses and were desperate to see the back of Puerto Madryn for good.

On returning to Trelew we continued 12 miles further west to the village of Gaiman. The Welsh had settled here, and unlike Puerto Madryn, Esquel and Trelew, you could not spend long in Gaiman without realising it.

The village had several Welsh tea houses, a museum portraying the Welshness of the area over the past 140 years, and every August

69

it hosts the Eisteddfodd, the Welsh Arts Festival. We saw the canal which the Welsh had built to provide water for farms. It had apparently worked well for the locals but a certain Mr. Peron nationalised it and charged people to use it. Not only did this cause consternation amongst the local populace but the Government also managed to make a loss on it.

We paid a visit, at his suggestion, to two of Ronnie Gough's aunts. They had lived in Gaiman all their lives but both spoke fluently in Spanish, English and Welsh. One of them showed us the local school – built in 1908, lessons had initially been taught in Welsh but after a period of closure it reopened in 1963 and Spanish then took over.

Gaiman proved to be an attractive little village to walk around. It had a lovely Plaza, lots of willow trees and the properties were mainly old red brick small houses or bungalows. The Italians had apparently come to Gaiman and their influence was certainly reflected in the architecture. The sisters were upset, and understandably so, by a recent trend for people to paint over the old brick, but were powerless to stop it.

They were as interested to know of our trip and of happenings in England as we were to know about them. We started to tell them of the incident with the knife in Cholila and, having got only as far as describing the men in the bar, one of them interjected: "Ah, Rene Griffiths". We could not believe it. They remembered him as a child, being brought up on a farm near Gaiman. One of their sons told us that Rene is a legend. He had heard so much about him yet had never met the man and wondered if he really existed.

If nothing else, the legend of Rene Griffiths demonstrates the closeness of the Welsh community. It is clearly a closeness not even broken by the hundreds of miles separating the settlements on the east and those developed some 25 years later on the west. We had enjoyed our time amongst them and in their tea houses but now it was time to move on.

Chapter 17

WE WANTED TO VISIT Tierra Del Fuego at the southernmost tip of Argentina. It is about 800 miles from Trelew. There is only one way to do it by road, through the Patagonian Desert. It is a deadly journey, we were told, through a flat changeless boring desert of low lying shrubs and only one town of any significance.

It would be a challenge and an experience to hitch hike it, but it could take four days or more, time was not on our side and the prospect, it must be said, did not exactly inspire us.

The other option was to fly. We went to Trelew Airport. There is only one Argentinian airline: Aerolineas Argentina. However we had been told that the Army airline, LADE, also took passengers and was much cheaper. We tried them first but they were full.

Then the bombshell came; yes, Aerolineas confirmed, they had a flight at midday and yes, they had seats, but the price had just gone up today.

We had been in Argentina long enough to know that this was serious: the increase would not be around the ten percent maximum you might expect, or at least accept, in Europe. Even so we had not quite prepared for the shock that was to come: the increase was 135 percent.

Having felt sure that we could do the journey for about £50 each, and with a chance of about £30 each, we were now faced with the prospect of spending £250 in one day. On our budget, to which we had through necessity been strictly adhering, that sum had to last over two weeks. There always has to be a degree of flexibility, but this much was out of the question.

It was the first – and indeed only – time that the extent of the misery of hyperinflation was really brought home to us; it seemed so unfair, so arbitrary and unplanned. To do anything in Argentina,

71

certainly to conduct business, must have been a nightmare. It was no wonder that many Argentinians seemed to have given up and were resorting to making money out of money by gambling on the exchange rate.

For perhaps 20 minutes we felt a sense of despair. Then we realised that we had to do something; there was always the bus, or perhaps, we thought, this was a message to us that we should be hitch hiking.

As we were contemplating these options, with a sense of reality though certainly not relish, a man approached us and asked if we were after a flight south. "I can take you on my Navy plane," he told us. This was surely too good to be true, but there was better to come, it will leave in half an hour, takes three hours and will cost the princely sum of £20 each.

It was a small plane seating perhaps one hundred people. The start was very bumpy; we wondered if the pilot was a trainee. The plane flew low and we had a very clear view of the patchwork, clearly defined green fields. It was not unlike arriving into England over Kent. Suddenly the green disappeared and there was simply a mass of light brown "nothingness" as far as the eye could see in any direction.

Later the coastline appeared to our left and shortly after that the desert disappeared from view and we could see only the ocean. Some way further south and about 400 miles to the east lie the Falkland Islands, but we never strayed far enough from the coast to even catch a glimpse.

Tierra Del Fuego, Spanish for "land of fire", is an island at the southern tip of Argentina and therefore also at the southern tip of South America. It is roughly the size of Scotland yet its two towns of any significance have populations of only around 25,000 people.

Our flight ended at one of them; Rio Grande. You could not help but be struck by the buildings; low and mainly wooden, many had corrugated iron roofs brightly painted in red, green or yellow whilst others were triangular shaped. Even the brick buildings seemed largely to have been painted. There was a "temporary" look about the place.

Rio Grande could be called an "oil town" having nearby at San Sebastian both the smallest and most southerly oil refinery in the world. It also seemed to us that it could be called a "shopping town". Considering its location half way down an island at the foot of a vast desert, it seemed remarkable to see the range and quality of goods on offer although whether anyone could actually afford them was another matter. We could not, and, there being nothing else in Rio Grande to distract us, we took a bus to the town at the bottom of the world.

Chapter 18

"ENJOY COCA-COLA" proclaimed the first poster we saw as we entered the town of Ushuaia.

Given that, after 1,000 miles or so of desert, followed by several hundred miles of remote island landscape, we had just reached the southernmost town in the world, and were now only 700 miles from Antarctica and 2,500 miles from the South Pole, it was hardly the welcome we would have expected. Clearly nowhere is sacred, no place too remote for the advertisers of that diabolical teeth-rotter.

Ushuaia's setting, its steeply rising streets sandwiched between the Beagle Channel to the south and mountains behind it to the north, is beautiful. The mountains beckoned and we answered the call. They literally engulf the town and we walked from the town centre to them.

The further back in the town we walked, the less solid looking the architecture became. Approaching the mountains, the roofs were of corrugated iron and the properties further apart. Many were wooden, all were very small, some were triangular and there were even buildings, presumably people's houses, which seemed to have been built on what looked like large copper rubbish bins.

We were quickly into the mountains, a thousand feet or so up, looking down on the scattered and varied buildings of Ushuaia and beyond out to the sea. It felt good to do a proper walk again, the first since El Bolson, and it was rejuvenating. It was also, however, bitterly cold. After April, we were told, this region is simply too cold to visit.

In contrast to its setting, the people of the town did not inspire. There seemed to be a notable absence of, or at least shortfall in, teeth, a fact not perhaps unrelated to the poster. The people carried worried expressions and had a generally unhealthy appearance. The fruit on offer was battered and bruised, the receptionist at our hotel did not appear to be able to write and there were a high number of stray dogs and stray children.

By far the greatest interest in Ushuaia lay in its history. The town has seen enormous changes in its population over the past 130 years. Back in the 1860s various Indian tribes lived on Tierra Del Fuego. They relied largely on fish, penguins and seals for nourishment and, according to some accounts, were not averse to supplementing their diet by eating each other.

Perhaps the finest account of the monumental changes which have taken place is contained in the story of E. Lucas Bridges entitled *Uttermost Part of the Earth*. Mr Bridges was born in Tierra Del Fuego in 1874 and died in 1949 only a year or so after completing his story.

The story of the English influence over the Indians in Tierra Del Fuego is the story of the Missionaries. Lucas Bridges' adoptive grandfather, one Reverend Despard, arranged for a man called Gardiner to join the Missionaries in the Falklands in 1854. Gardiner went on to Tierra Del Fuego. He tried unsuccessfully to persuade the local Indians to go to the Falklands.

He did however take one of the Indians, a young man who was called Jeremy Button, back to England for a few years of Christianising and Civilisation.

Button was subsequently returned to his native land where, the missionaries intended, he would teach his fellow Indians both the importance of Christianity and also lots of more down to earth things such as how to eat with a knife and fork.

Gardiner was determined to set up a mission on Tierra Del Fuego. The missionaries built the first church on the island and in 1859 the great day arrived; the first ever Christian Church Service on Tierra Del Fuego.

To say that it was a set back for the missionaries would be something of an understatement. What actually happened was that, just as the Service was beginning, the Indians suddenly launched a vicious attack on the missionaries clubbing, stoning and spearing them to death.

There was only one survivor, a man called Alfred Cole, who had been discovered by a search party. Cole blamed the whole thing on Button; Button in turn laid the blame squarely at the feet of the Ona Indians, a tribe of foot Indians with whom it was generally considered that it was not a very good idea to mess.

This catastrophe led Reverend Despard to report back to the Patagonian Missionary Society in England that the attempts at "spreading the word" in Tierra Del Fuego did not appear to be going down too well with the local populace. Indeed he went as far as recommending that the attempt be abandoned. The response of the Society, received some two years later, was that in the circumstances it seemed best to, in effect, cut and run.

However the missionaries did not. Reverend Despard left, but his adoptive sons Thomas Bridges, Lucas' father, then only 18, chose to stay. The relationship between the missionaries and the Indians did improve although it is difficult to imagine that it could have done anything else.

Thomas Bridges first visited Tierra Del Fuego in 1863 with a man called Stirling. He had by then obtained a reasonable grasp of the Indian dialect. This was important; Lucas Bridges claims in his book that mistakes were made by the English as a result of misunderstandings and further that this has also resulted in certain myths being handed down to succeeding generations.

The story that the Indians engaged in cannibalism, passed down by, amongst others, Charles Darwin is, according to Lucas Bridges, a fallacy based on misunderstanding, either by the Indians of the question if it was in English, or by Darwin and others if the answer was in the Indian dialect. Is it inconceivable, I wonder, that the Indians had more intelligence than is generally credited to them and, tired of endless questioning by these white infiltrators and do gooders, decided to make up a story that they killed and ate each other?

Stirling and Bridges spent much of their time on the island and in 1871 Bridges moved there permanently. Ushuaia, which in the native tongue means "inner harbour to the westward" was considered a prime site for development on account of its large sheltered harbour, its relatively easy access by ship and its cultivatable land.

Vegetables were planted, homes were built out of wood and corrugated iron and a mission residence called Stirling House was constructed.

It was difficult to stir the Indians into action to assist with the planting and the building, but over time, Lucas Bridges explains, the town developed and the Indians became less hostile and more civilised.

The transition from a population made up entirely of primitive Indian tribes living largely off the sea to today's population has been gradual but dramatic, and the circle, if it can be so called, is now complete.

There is today not a single Indian left on the island. An entire race has died out in around four generations. The introduction to the fourth edition of Lucas Bridges' book published in 1963 states that there were then only a few hundred Indians left, measles having accounted for most of them. Now, less than 140 years after they had the island to themselves, they are part of history.

Chapter 19

WHEN OUR PLANE left the runway of Ushuaia's tiny airport, we were heading north for the first time on the journey. It was March 14th 1990; two months had passed since leaving Rio de Janeiro. We had covered perhaps 5,000 miles, the distance as the crow flies from Rio to Ushuaia being a little over half of that.

I had to be back at work on June 7th. We were determined to go overland, to travel the length of South, then Central America and then through Mexico and finally up the West coast of the States into Canada to our final destination, Vancouver. Effectively, therefore, between now and the start of June, we had to cover some 12,000 miles. There would not be a lot of time for hanging around. In short we had to get a move on.

When the plane first headed off it flew eastwards. We went over the Beagle Channel and could see islands to our right, the islands south even of Tierra Del Fuego beyond which lay Antarctica. Quickly we started heading north, and were over mainland Argentina and back to the view of brown "nothingness" that was the desert.

The first half of the flight did nothing to prepare us for what was in store. The transition from desert to snow capped mountains and lakes was as extraordinary as it was sudden. We were flying low and had a clear and quite fantastic view. The town of Calafate into which we were flying looked tiny next to the vast mountain ranges around it and Lake Argentino next to which it nestles.

Calafate is a small town of 3,000 inhabitants. It was only a five minute walk from the airport to the "town centre". The reason for visiting it was simple: it is the starting point for a visit to one of the most incredible glaciers in the world and one of the few that is still growing.

The glacier, called Ventisquero Moreno, is some 50 miles away. We took a guided tour, in practice the only way to see it. Ventisquero Moreno lies at the junction of two lakes, Lake Argentino and Lake Rico. Ice from the mountains above the lakes falls into the water and the water is so cold that it remains as ice. The vast block of ice which forms stretches forward for around three miles from the start of the mountain, moves forward by about 100 metres every year and is roughly 60 metres high above the the surface of the water.

The ice which is furthest from the mountains blocks the flow of water from Lake Rico into Lake Argentino. However, such is the pressure from the water below that over time the lower part of the ice breaks leaving only the ice above it forming a "bridge of ice".

Every three to four years the build up of pressure is so immense that the bridge and all the ice around it also break. Incredibly, from the gun shot like sounds which the pressure creates and which herald the start of this break to the end can easily take 24 hours. People travel thousands of miles to see it and, judging from the film we saw of it, remain spellbound throughout. Many described it as the greatest experience of their life.

We were not fortunate enough to witness it, the previous occurrence having been too recent, but we certainly heard rumblings and saw movement and blocks of ice falling 60 metres or so into the water.

After the "high" of the glacier we were very quickly brought back to reality. The journey from Calafate into Chile was atrocious. The distance from Calafate to the Chilean border is perhaps 30 miles. Our journey took 17 hours and when it had finished we were about 100 miles further South than when we had started. To make any progress into Chile, we had first to go backwards.

The fault is Chile's: the islands, lakes, national parks and mountains which make up Southern Chile are, everyone told us and we were shortly to see it for ourselves, quite beautiful. Yet it makes travelling from one place to another something of a nightmare if you are on a tight schedule. The only flight from Calafate into Chile was fully booked and there was no direct bus. We had to take the 7.15 am bus to a place called La Experanza which comprised nothing but one cafe. We arrived there at 9.30 am and the idea was then to pick up the so called connecting bus to Rio Turbo. The trouble was that nobody seemed to know exactly when this connecting bus would arrive and general opinion was that it would be between 4.00 and 5.00 pm.

I was saved from severe depression by Jonathan Raban's *Foreign Land* but Jo was not put in the best of moods by what she saw (and it was hard to dispute it) as a wasted day. The bus finally arrived at 5.30 pm. It had green seats, many of which were split, and the only space was in the back row alongside a pregnant lady, two young children and a baby. Neither this nor the flat and monotonous route did anything to cheer us. I think I continued with *Foreign Land* whilst Jo persisted in cursing the situation which really now that we were moving was not too disastrous.

We finally reached the border at Rio Turbo at about 10.00 pm. We then had to take another connecting bus. Fortunately this connection was not as loose as the one before and, even better, was going directly to Puerto Natales. The border crossing could not have been easier and all in all things were finally looking up.

On arrival in Puerto Natales, we perused our ever reliable *South American Handbook* for accommodation and selected one, on account, I think mainly, of its cheapness. It was a long walk and when we reached the address to discover that there was nothing there, Jo's uncharacteristic and short-lived misery was complete. We wandered somewhat uncertainly in the dark until an English and Swiss chap approached us in the street with a strong recommendation: living in the house of a lovely Chilean lady. "It's two US dollars per night including breakfast," said the Swiss, with an enthusiasm which made me think, correctly as it transpired, that he must have come from the German speaking part of Switzerland.

We went. It was now after midnight. A smiling Chilean lady greeted us cheerfully with a "Bon Dia," and we chatted briefly. We were struck by how friendly she was at this late hour. Our first impression of Chile was a good one.

Chapter 20

THE LADY in whose house we were staying was a lively lady of perhaps 60 years. She seemed to thrive on, and be kept youthful by, housing and feeding, not to mention entertaining, around 20 travellers, most easily young enough to be her children.

We breakfasted in her kitchen on home made bread, rhubarb and plum jam and instant coffee and spent the rest of the day barely venturing more than a few feet from the Aga, eating a succession of delicious meals and conversing with the steady stream of others fortunate enough to be staying there.

One was Japanese. This was most unusual, not so much because we hadn't seen Japanese travellers before, but because they always seem to travel in large packs and we had thought them incapable of doing anything on their own. This one was the exception, a rebel perhaps. His English was very shaky; his Spanish non-existent. How he got around was a mystery to us all.

"Where did you start your trip?" somebody asked. This was greeted, as were all questions first time up, with a look of puzzlement, followed by a wide eyed expression and a raised finger. The first signified that he hadn't understood the question, the second that he suddenly had, even though generally it had not been necessary to repeat it.

"Lima," he replied.

Lima is reputedly one of the most dangerous cities in South America. General opinion is that you should not even think about going there; if you know someone there and can speak fluent Spanish, you may survive but otherwise forget it. Yet this young man, never previously out of Japan, knowing nobody in South America, and with not a word of Spanish and only pidgin English, chose to travel around South America and selected Lima as his point of arrival. There is a thin line between gusto and stupidity but this Japanese, and perhaps among his nationality he is not alone, seemed blissfully ignorant of it.

Somebody asked him his name. Again the bewildered look, followed by an indication of understanding and then the answer: "Suzuki." We thought that maybe he had misunderstood: out came his passport as proof: yes, his name clearly was Suzuki.

"Where do you live in Japan?" someone else asked. He told us he came from Toyota. At this, even the German in the kitchen was struggling to contain himself.

And then, warming to his theme, Suzuki told us that his family name is Honda. It was some minutes before any of us could talk again. Throughout, Suzuki sat in stony silence, a look of bewilderment etched all over his face, until he said to us, with a wry smile: "but nothing is Yamaha."

So he had understood, finally if not from the start. He had reduced a group of various nationalities nearly to tears, united them in laughter. What's more he had done it in a language he could hardly speak. Anyone who can do that is perhaps entitled to treat backpacking around South America as something of a doddle.

After a day which could hardly have been less lazy, albeit one that had been very enjoyable and a wonderful introduction to Chilean hospitality and food, we were ready to witness some of the Chilean scenery about which we had heard so much.

Chapter 21

IF ANY COUNTRY in this Continent can lay claim to being the "in" place of the 90s for travellers, then that country is Chile. "Just wait till you get to Chile," endless backpackers had enthused, "fantastic scenery, wonderful people, delicious food, safe as houses and incredibly inexpensive.".

Such was their enthusiasm, we feared that it could hardly fail to disappoint. Torres del Paine, one of Chile's 50 National Parks, certainly did not. If anything, it surpassed even our very high expectations.

As in many other countries, in contrast to England where people live and work within the National Parks, Chilean National Parks are areas of wilderness. Generally the only people that live within them are people connected with running the parks. The Torres del Paine National Park, a few hours bus ride from Puerto Natales, is slightly smaller in area than the Yorkshire Dales National Park within which surely lies some of England's remotest countryside. You can feel isolation and peace and beauty in the Dales but sooner or later you will come across a village or at least an old disused stone farm building (not that there is anything wrong with that). In the Torres del Paine National Park you can walk for days and not see a building.

What you do see is a spectacular, at times breathtaking, blend of snow-clad mountain peaks, glaciers, lakes and waterfalls amongst lush green fields as far as the eye can see in all directions. We also saw hares and ostriches, herds of guanacos were roaming everywhere, and above us the occasional condor would glide past.

We spent only a day in the Park, barely able to take in the beauty of it all, and if we have any one regret arising from the entire trip it is that our schedule was by now too tight to allow a longer stay.

Many were spending one or two weeks there. A New Zealander, who returned with us on the bus to Puerto Natales, had taken enough food supposedly for a week, and, despite running out after five days, had then spent three further days walking around in what must have been a weak and hungry state because he simply could not bear to leave. He was ill afterwards but no doubt would have considered it a small price to pay.

From Puerto Natales, as indeed from everywhere now until we reached Vancouver, we had to head North. Once again the geography of Chile created a problem. In order to progress north, we would have firstly to go south; 150 miles south to be precise, to a town called Punta Arenas. From there, we had been informed, we could either take a boat or a bus heading north.

Punta Arenas in Chilean Patagonia is Chile's southernmost city, and, with a population of 100,000 inhabitants, was the largest city we had been to since Buenos Aires some seven weeks before. Its buildings, like those in Puerto Natales, seemed to be largely wooden or corrugated iron. It was not at first sight a city which could be said to inspire.

Our first concern, with all due respect to Punta Arenas, was to find out how to get out of it. We were still some 1,500 miles south of Santiago as the crow flies (which meant a lot more travelling miles). The plane was too dear. The boat would not leave for several days and would take about four days to reach Puerto Montt, some 1,000 miles north. The bus would leave the next morning and take 33 hours to reach the same destination.

Although, again on account of geography and lack of roads, the bus journey would take us back over to the east coast of Argentina and through many of our old haunts, it was, given our rushed and impecunious state, the only serious option.

First, however, despite its lack of promise, we would take a look at Punta Arenas. Somebody had recommended the cemetery. Our initial feeling was to think that it said little for a town if its cemetery was its greatest attraction. This soon changed when we saw it.

The dead of Punta Arenas clearly lived in style, if you pardon the expression. Far from being scrunched up in the soil with a small tombstone above them proclaiming that they were "much loved", these people had their own little rooms, perhaps 10 feet high, with

84

shelves on either side and a table at the back. There was a locked entrance door, but presumably close friends and relatives had a key. On a table were flowers, candles and photographs of what we assumed to be the deceased and their relatives. One of the shelves generally held the coffin, the other was usually left free, perhaps for visitors to sit on.

We noticed that a number of the deceased were Yugoslavs; some were British. An elderly American couple informed us that the town had been established by Yugoslavs. It transpired that they were great cemetery goers.

"Wherever we go", they told us, "we always visit them. The history of a place is in its cemetery."

Apart from the cemetery, my other main memory of Punta Arenas is of lunch. Even by Chilean standards, it was wonderful.

We had a national dish as a starter; caldillo de congrio. I have on several occasions nearly, and on one occasion actually, been thrown out of an English restaurant for complaining that the "home-made soup" is in fact out of a packet or tin. My requests on such occasions to "have a word" with the chef as to how he made it have met with either stony silence or aggression. I cannot imagine that caldillo de congrio has ever been the subject of such disquiet.

It comprises a large piece of conger eel, onions, carrots, potatoes and, the piece de resistance, fresh coriander. You can taste the freshness and naturalness with every mouthful. Alongside the hot and sour soups of Thailand and the Russian Borscht, it must surely rank amongst the world's great soups. A piece of succulent salmon and potatoes for main course and several glasses of pisco sour – roughly equivalent to Vodka and lemon – completed a memorable occasion. The meal was rounded off with coffee. In stark contrast to Argentina where you are provided with a small cup and saucer into which immaculate waiters pour fresh coffee, a Chilean after dinner coffee could hardly be more down to earth. A waitress in ordinary clothing deposits a mug, boiled water and a huge tin of Nescafe in front of you and you are left to get on with it.

We were left feeling up to nothing more than sitting in a local cinema which we duly did, watching *Planes, Trains, and Automobiles* which was worth seeing and *Honey I shrunk the Kids* which certainly was not.

85

Chapter 22

THE NEXT DAY started for us at 6.00 am. It was hard to imagine that an entire day's travelling could be all deadly but it was.

We were soon back into Argentina, crossing Patagonia from west to east once again. The previous time it had been dark; judging from this route, admittedly considerably further south, we had missed nothing. It was flat, dry and unchanging. Apart from a few trees there were just the usual low lying shrubs with which we had unfortunately become all too familiar. Our spirits were probably at their highest point when we were in Rio Gallegos on the east side of Patagonia having quite a good lunch (although not good enough to go into details) and watching Argentina's wonder girl Gabriella Sabatini playing a girl called Fernandez on the restaurant television.

The bus was of high quality; we had reclining seats, foot rests, wash rooms, blankets, curtains and on bus entertainment. We could have done without the entertainment; the only film that was in English was about a horse that could talk and gave advice to a stock broker. Unfortunately, unlike on aeroplanes, the volume was there whether you wanted it or not. Fortunately the entertainment finally ended and after a complimentary pisco sour we spent the next seven hours or so in darkness catching periodic winks of sleep as the bus ploughed on through the night.

When we awoke, it was around 6.30 am and we were passing through El Bolson, scene of our Andes climb, and a place, like many others on this journey, to which we had not expected to return.

Ninety miles or so and five hours later, after bumping along the same stony, windy road we had previously used in the other direction, we were passing the outskirts of Bariloche. It was a shock; the Lake was not visible and indeed little was but small shanty towns. How different to our first impression of this delightful town and how misleading it would have been to anyone on the bus seeing it for the first time.

An hour or two later having spent about 15 miles seemingly in no man's land, we finally returned into Chile and reached our destination, Puerto Montt, that afternoon. Puerto Montt was established by Germans in 1852. This may account for it being rather orderly and solid-looking, certainly in comparison with the typical Chilean town. From what we had seen so far, although Chile had many attractions, its architecture could not be said to be amongst them. Puerto Montt was at least a relative improvement.

Coincidentally we met a German there; a girl whom we had first seen in the Torres del Paine National Park, who had flown from Puerto Natales and took great delight in telling us that it had cost her only 10,000 pesos (£30) because "a friend works for the airline".

"You only just arrived here?" she asked us, clearly hoping that we had. We told her of our journey. She made a very poor attempt at looking sympathetic.

"So I had two more days than you in Punta Arenas but I arrive here before you," she went on, displaying the subtlety of a bull in a china shop, "that's funny." Hilarious, we thought.

"And here," she continued, "I am staying in hotel for 1,500 pesos. Then I will stay north of here. I have a friend so I can stay for free." And off she went, no doubt looking for the cheapest meal in Puerto Montt or a new found friend who could do her a financial favour.

The highlight of Puerto Montt was a small fishing port called Angelmo, a short walk from the town centre. Weather beaten, wrinkled fishermen were hunched over buckets cleaning and shelling the day's catch; there were endless tiny restaurants which could each sit about six people and where you could, and we did, sample bowls of crabs, mussels, sea urchins, chicken and potatoes in a sauce, and where artisans sold a range of wares including wood carvings and alpaca.

A six hour bus ride through lush countryside which came as close to English landscape as anything we had seen so far led us to the city of Temuco. For reasons not of its own making, the memory of Temuco will unfortunately always be with me.

It was March 25th 1990. My diary showed that it was Mothers Day in the UK. It was also exactly three months since I had last phoned home. I cannot bear the telephone at the best of times but to phone home from so far away can be a nightmare. You have one eye on the clock and there is so much to say but you don't know where to start. Ludicrous though it is, such conversations seem to start with a discussion on the weather and invariably end all too abruptly leaving both participants feeling somewhat cold.

"Hello, mum it's me." My mother sounded uncharacteristically slow on the uptake but given that it was 1.00 am British time this was perhaps understandable.
"Happy Mothers Day. Sorry to ring so late but the bus has only just arrived."
"Oh, thank you, how are you?"
"Fine, thanks, we're having a good time."
To an eavesdropper it must have sounded as if I had just caught the last bus home after a night at the local disco. "How are you?"
"Yes, fine."
I remember thinking that there was a hesitation in my mother's voice, and then she continued.
"One piece of sad news is that Granny has died."

I still recall those words, those exact words. The rest was really only a blur . . . I staggered out of the phone booth, fell onto Jo, who must have done well to remain upright, and could not contain myself.

Words were beyond me; how lucky I was that Jo was not. My Granny was 80; Jo and I and all my family and several of my grandparents' lifelong friends had celebrated her 80th birthday the July before in their garden. She had looked as if she had loved it as she loved any social gathering. I had seen her just before leaving, and although not in the best of health, I had not dared to think the unthinkable, that I would never see her again.

Memories of the 27 years we had shared flooded back; the Christmases she always made such fun, Junior tennis tournaments and trips to Wimbledon, the silver sweet trolley of my childhood visits, replaced as I grew older by a glass or two of sherry. At one

88

time, notably when taking A Levels and later Law College finals, my grandparents' home was the only place I could truly relax.

There had been 100 people at the funeral. My grandfather, the other half of a remarkable double act, had apparently overcome the shock and returned to the cheery optimistic outlook with which he had breezed through life for the past 86 years.

Goodbye Granny. This book is for you. How I wish you could have read it.

Chapter 23

THE NEXT DAY, although, or perhaps because, it was my 28th birthday and with my Granny in my thoughts, I had a temporary feeling that all this was so futile; here we are in another town that has neither incredible beauty nor great interest. What is the point of it all? In general I prefer to get on with things than to analyse them deeply. Jo is a great doer in her own way but can analyse and agonise herself into depression. Normally I cannot. In Temuco I did.

Jo took me off to the Temuco cattle auction in the hope of ending this unfamiliar state of affairs.

The first striking thing about the Temuco cattle auction was that it had no cattle. There were, however, pigs and sheep. I was appalled by the cruelty with which they appeared to be treated. If a pig did not leave its pen it was "encouraged" to do so by being struck fiercely by a man with a pointed stick. There were some 10 pigs per pen and generally when one had been struck some of the others followed tamely. Equally if one pig managed to avoid the stick, the others would follow his route. The net result was that most of them were beaten fairly unpleasantly before leaving the pen to start a new life.

It was perhaps the comparison with the life of the pigs that renewed my enthusiasm to get on with things. The first thing we got on with was lunch: a solid soup or liquid stew called cazuela de ave, a typical Chilean dish comprising large pieces of chicken, potatoes, rice, onions and peppers: quite delicious.

With both body and soul restored, we took the afternoon bus to Pucon. Not only was this edging ever closer to Santiago, but it was also the starting point for a climb up the active Villarica volcano.

Amazingly enough, there are some 12,000 volcanoes in Chile of which around 50 are active.

We arrived at the hostel to be greeted by several other travellers who had just returned from the climb which had taken them all day. Whilst there were still sulphur fumes at the summit, we were told, there had not been an eruption for many years so, "there's really nothing to worry about".

Guide, boots, crampons and ice-axes arranged, we woke the next morning in eager anticipation. Our hopes were to be dashed. It was not so much the fact that it had rained but that the visibility was virtually non existent that led our guide to say that the climb could not be undertaken.

We changed our bus tickets to the next day and then, as the day went on without improvement and locals told us that once it rained it doesn't stop for days, decided that time did not allow an indefinite wait and changed them back again.

Whilst waiting in the hostel that afternoon, we heard someone saying: "My older brother told me that when in Peru, you've got to kill them before they kill you."

It was not just what was said that made us prick up our ears; the voice sounded familiar. We went into the kitchen – it was non other than Big Al, the Canadian truck driver we had previously seen on the east coast of Argentina.

Big Al seemed to have a never ending fund of stories for the entertainment of fellow travellers. That afternoon, amongst others, he told us of a confrontation with a grisly bear when he was travelling in Alaska and of being what he thought was hopelessly lost whilst alone on a walking expedition.

"I was lost, man. I had to get on my hands and knees, and I crawled, literally, for over an hour with my ruck sack on my back. Boy was I relieved to reach a road. And, do you know, when I reached it, I realised that all that time I had been crawling along, I'd been parallel to a path about 15 yards away."

That evening we took yet another night bus. Some 12 hours after setting off, we came to. It was light and we were in the outskirts of Santiago.

On arrival at the main station, we took a tube into the centre, but the accommodation that we had been recommended – a former mansion with Victorian furniture – was full. We then made what turned out to be a not terribly sensible decision to walk to the Tourist Office.

There were two reasons why this was a bad decision. Firstly, it involved a walk of about a mile loaded down with luggage, along Avenida O'Higgins, one of Santiago's main streets. I knew little about Santiago, but I did know that, on account of being surrounded by mountains, it has a terrible smog problem. Had we not been aware of this before arriving, we soon would have been. The incessant noise and traffic fumes as we walked that mile or so hardly endeared us to the city.

Secondly, the Tourist Office recommendation could hardly have been more disastrous. The lady there seemed helpful enough and arranged for us to stay in a "Casa" (a Chilean home). Many breaths of smog later, we were there.

An unfriendly looking lady who must have been in her sixties let us in. As I passed the loo on the way to our bedroom, the door was open and an extremely old lady was in there standing up over the loo seat with her skirt down. It was not easy to ignore it, but we continued into the bedroom.

As I was just asking Jo if she had seen the old lady in the loo, she (by which I mean the lady who had been in the loo) came into our room.

Her legs were like sticks, her face just a mass of wrinkles.

She looked at least 90 and, if it is possible to say it of someone over 90, had not aged well. It was a wonder she was still alive and even more of a wonder that she could transport herself from the loo to the bedroom.

She started shouting aggressively at us in what we assumed was Spanish. She was totally incoherent and clearly quite mad. The other lady shouted "Mama," at her a few times but otherwise did nothing.

If it is possible in such a situation to say that anything could amount to a saving grace, then the saving grace here was that the old lady had at least managed to pull her skirt back up.

Jo could not stand it, and I cannot say that I was too chuffed either. We said that we did not want to stay.

"You must pay," responded the younger one. We refused. "OK, you must pay 2,000 pesos."

Again, we refused, and decided just to leave, which we duly did, amongst a tirade of abuse from the younger woman and a tirade of incoherent nonsense from the older.

Fortunately, after some searching, we eventually found a good hotel with double bedroom and private bathroom for a little under £5 each and set off to wander the streets of Santiago determined not to be too prejudiced by our first impression.

Santiago's setting is reputedly beautiful, high above sea level with the snow-capped Andes mountain range in view. Sadly it was overcast for most of our two days there and we could see little beyond the city centre.

A short walk led us to the Plaza de Armas, a quite delightful square in the heart of the city. There were trees and benches and a large water fountain, people strolled through the square at a somewhat more leisurely pace than along Avenida O'Higgins, and it was a welcome escape from the noise and bustle. On one side of the square lies a Cathedral, on another a lovely colonial building which is now the Central Post Office, and on the other two sides, a large indoor shopping market.

In the Cathedral, a middle-aged lady handed me a religious book written of course in Spanish and asked me to read it and write to her with my comments. I told her that my Spanish was not good enough and/or that I had insufficient time, but she was almost manic in her insistence and was clearly not the full shilling.

Two fruit cakes within about four hours of arriving was beginning to make us wonder about the inhabitants of Santiago, but we met no more and perhaps were just unfortunate. There was a fair amount of crying going on in the Cathedral but we put this down to religious, rather than general, mania.

The Plaza de Armas seemed to be Santiago's highlight. My overall impression of the city was that, whilst it had some very fine buildings, particularly Georgian and Victorian, there was no escaping the fact that it is a noisy, polluted, bustling and fairly dirty and rundown city.

I am not a lover of cities at the best of times, and at four million inhabitants, its population exceeded by about 3.9 million the size of city which I generally find appealing. We were not too distressed by the prospect of leaving.

Chapter 24

OUR BUS JOURNEY to the border town of Arica took around 16 hours. The distance was a little under half of Chile's length and we were heading north, parallel to the Pacific Ocean, for the entire journey.

Unusually, the bus was only about half full. Most of our fellow passengers were either young ladies with babies or fairly elderly men.

The bus itself was not quite as clean or as spacious as those to which we had become accustomed, but there were the usual W.C. facilities and a video providing regular "entertainment". Two men shared the driving, which again was usual for significant journeys, and there was also a supervisor/general assistant on board.

We were quickly out of Santiago. I recall being struck by the smartness of northern Santiago; we generally found that the northern sectors of South American cities were poor and rundown. On departing the city, we were into a lush green landscape of farms and vineyards (much of Chile's acclaimed wines are produced near Santiago) and of gentle hills with mountains in the distance.

After an early lunch of chicken, rice, beetroot, cucumber, bread and apple for desert, I fell asleep and I think Jo did too. When we awoke, the scenery had altered drastically. It was not unlike Patagonia, although thankfully more interesting. The low lying shrubs and thorns were similar, but the road less straight, the landscape generally more hilly and there were even mountains in the distance.

Later, after passing nearby the town of La Serena, some 300 miles north of Santiago, we travelled through an area of huge brown hills, rocks and valleys where the road regularly turned sharply giving an ever-changing panorama.

95

The area is classified as semi-desert, an area for which the Chileans had successfully fought a war against Peru and Bolivia, primarily for its importance as a source of copper and nitrate. It was clearly not an area in which you could have many people living.

After some hours, we stopped at a fruit stall which might just as well have been called a papaya stall: there was papaya honey, papaya on a stick, papaya juice and chopped papaya in little bags. It seemed odd to find a tropical fruit in the desert and it was not at all clear where the vendors lived.

During the night, as the bus continued relentlessly on through what was now full, rather than semi, desert, we were awoken by spluttering noises.

It sounded like a child but was in fact a man, quite an elderly man, who was seemingly struggling to breath. The lights came on and the supervisor on the bus and one of the passengers pushed and punched him whilst a girl shook his head. I was not convinced that they knew what they were doing but I knew that I could do no better and left them to it, feeling that I really ought to learn basic first aid. The man looked fairly unhealthy but I was pleased to note that he was still alive the next morning.

That morning, we journeyed through a flat sand desert, the like of which we had not previously experienced in South America. There were no rocks, no mountains or hills, and no vegetation. Apparently it is an area in which it never rains.

A dreadful American film about some children who wanted a condemned building to remain so that they could do break-dancing around it, was showing. It made both Jo and me cringe many times, most of all when a girl of perhaps 12 years addressed her parents as "you guys".

We reached Arica at lunch time. This border town of 145,000 people was like nothing we had yet seen on the trip. Full of markets and street vendors, it had a friendly buzz about it and seemed far more Asian in character than South American.

Not for the first time, our prime concern on arrival was to try to sort out how to depart. We were not even entirely sure where we would depart to. Arica is within a short ride of Peru, but is also possible to go to La Paz, the Bolivian capital, and try to work out a route heading north from there.

The route through Peru was clearly the more direct and simple; the problem was that everyone was telling us that it was too dangerous.

That the British Embassy advised us not to go would not in itself have worried us overly, but the fact that fellow travellers, who do not necessarily err on the side of caution, were saying the same thing made us sit up and take notice.

Matters were made even worse by the imminence of the Peruvian General Election which it was thought could turn the country into a blood bath.

Obtaining information was not easy. The Tourist Office thought that there was a train to La Paz in three days' time; there was nobody at the station, but a notice indicated that the next train was not for another ten days.

The lady at our hostel helpfully informed us that a lorry driver friend could give us a lift to La Paz the next day. At least it seemed it was helpful until he didn't turn up.

"All these lorries start from one spot," a local informed us, "they go one way for Bolivia and another way for Peru."

We wasted several hours there.

"It's better tomorrow morning," one driver told us.
"Tonight at 6.00 pm is the best time," said another.
"It's impossible to hitch hike," said the lady at the tourist office.

After a wasted day, we became sufficiently desperate to enquire about flying, but, as anticipated, the cost ruled it out.

Although she had made it fairly clear that going through Peru was not yet an option, I gently broached with Jo the possibility of doing just that. It was not just that I had set my heart on doing the whole journey over land, but that there really did not seem to be any other practical way of heading north.

We made enquiries. This involved a lot of to-ing and fro-ing and took a morning, but finally we found that we could take a taxi to the Peruvian border. The other big advantage of doing this, we were told, was that the driver would take our passports and deal with customs and avoid the hours of delay which otherwise travellers would be likely to endure. Our only concern about this was that the person who had told us it was the driver himself.

An elderly Canadian man approached us and gave our driver the seal of approval.

"I live here for half the year. This one's O.K.," he assured us. We wondered if he'd ever been to Peru.

"Oh, no," he replied indignantly, "I don't need to do that sort of thing," which made us think that we didn't either but by now we'd reached the point of no return.

"Be careful," he continued, "two Canadians were robbed recently and the robbers broke their legs to stop them going to the Police Station."

How he knew that that was why they had broken them was beyond us, but it was hardly the send off we were after. And then, somewhat incongruously in view of what he had just told us, he said "well, enjoy your trip," and off he went.

And off we went too. We were quickly back into the sand desert, and within 15 minutes or so, had reached the Chilean border. Our driver seemed friendly with the officials and we were soon on the move again, apparently in "No man's land".

The Peruvian frontier was only a short way ahead. This delayed us longer but not as long, I am sure, as it would have done without our driver who again seemed to be on back-slapping terms with the officials.

By almost all accounts, we were not only now in the Continent's most dangerous country, but had reached it, with the General Election only five days away, at the most lethal possible time.

Chapter 25

PERU IS LONG AND THIN. In comparison with Chile, it is short and broad, but by any normal standards, it is long and thin. Lima, the capital city, is a little under half way up the Pacific coast, roughly 600 miles north of the border.

Our aim was simple: to get through Peru in the quickest possible time. Reports that guerrilla movements were periodically stopping long distance buses and shooting its occupants to prevent them voting were somewhat worrying to say the least. Our theory was that the chance of this would increase as the Election neared.

We took a bus from the border to a town called Tacna. We were very anxious: the *South American Handbook* issued a warning about Tacna, describing it as "one of the worst towns for robberies, particularly around the bus station at night".

We steeled ourselves on arrival; had we not read this, we would not have thought it, for Tacna seemed a pleasant town. There were street vendors everywhere. The people had noticeably darker skins and were more Indian looking than the Chileans, and their faces were smiling and cheerful.

Fortunately the bus took us to the station from which the Lima bus would leave. We took the precaution of tying all our bags together in the hope of thwarting thieves. It made carrying them awkward but this was a small price to pay.

We arrived at 3.45 and prayed that there would be a bus to Lima very soon. There was; the next one was at 4.00 pm but, unbelievably, there were no tickets left.

"When's the next one?" I asked in desperation.

"4.00 pm on Wednesday."

"Wednesday?" That is two days away, we cannot wait two days here, I thought.

This was devastating news. I tried to appear calm to Jo but rarely have I felt so desperate; I would have given anything to be on that bus. We told the man at the ticket counter that we would sit on the floor or stand or do anything, but please, just let us on that bus.

Just as it seemed that all hope was lost, the man at the ticket counter produced one ticket. I was not sure how, or why, but I grabbed it with glee.

After some discussion, he seemed agreeable to my boarding the bus without a ticket. Again, I was not sure why, but it was not the time for questions.

Only then did another problem dawn on us: we had no Peruvian currency.

"Can we pay in dollars?"

Our temporary saviour laughed, wondering perhaps how much further backwards he was going to have to bend over before we were satisfied. This problem was also resolved with good humour, and we dragged our luggage by the string tied round it towards the bus.

I felt a tap on my shoulder. It was our saviour: a girl had just handed her ticket in, another 12 dollars and its mine. Rarely have I parted with money with such speed or enthusiasm.

There was what could only be described as an unceremonious scramble for seats as we boarded the bus. Ours were only four from the front, and, more importantly, as we hoped for views of the Pacific coastline, on the left hand side.

The bus finally departed about an hour late. In Brazil and Argentina, we had become accustomed to buses leaving on the dot. In Peru, we were led to believe, if your bus leaves only an hour late, you count yourself lucky.

The bus itself also left much to be desired. It had no light, the WC was permanently locked, several people were standing, leg room hardly existed and in general it had a shoddy, second-hand feel about it.

It was mainly women on board, generally with a child or children in one arm and a sack of unknown contents in the other.

They looked the sort of people who could tolerate hardship. Their faces were hard and worn; their babies suggested that they were in their twenties or thirties although they could have passed for many years more.

The flat, sandy landscape of the early stages gave way to the deserted Pacific coastline, rocks and hills, sand dunes and sharp bends, and even occasionally, and surprisingly, a little grass.

The journey was broken by frequent, short stops when street vendors appeared, seemingly from nowhere, and people disembarked to purchase a selection of avocados, sweetcorn, ice cream, soft drinks and bread. These were loud, scrappy, occasions; the vendors seemed to think that they could not secure a sale without permanently shrieking the names of the items on offer, even though these items were clear for all to see.

A man on the bus was standing reading a newspaper. We could not help but be struck by the headline; "Military take control of Lima." Concern for our safety got the better of us.

"Is it safe in Lima?" we asked him.
"Oh yes, very tranquil," came his rather surprising response.
"But aren't the Army in control?"
"Only at night, during the day the normal Police are in control, but anyway it's safer with the Army there."

Although he had not convinced us, he had at least reduced our sense of panic.

It was dark by around 7.30, and, there being no lights on the bus, we spent as much as possible of the next 11 hours or so asleep, as the bus struggled on through the desert.

We were greeted on waking by the most spectacular scenery of the journey: travelling around hairpin bends with the Ocean to our left, and hills and dramatic rock formations to the right.

Shortly afterwards, we reached the attractive little fishing village of Chala. Although only a village, it was far and away the biggest settlement we had seen since leaving Tacna some 14 hours before.

Chala marked the halfway point of the trip; we still had 400 miles, a full day's travelling, ahead of us, although the worst of it, namely the night time, was at least behind us.

The next main stop was at the town of Nazca. There was nothing remarkable about the town itself, but there is something very remarkable only 15 miles away: the Nazca Lines.

The Nazca Lines are a succession of lines cut into the stony desert. Some of the Lines are straight, but others form specific shapes such as the shape of a dog, birds and a tree. It is not known exactly who put them there, nor when.

They have inevitably attracted much research. General opinion is that three different groups could be responsible for them: the Paracas people from 900 to 22 BC, the Nazcas from 200 BC to AD 600 and the settlers from Ayacucho in around AD 630.

The question of what they represent is more controversial. Views range from the Lines representing a huge astronomical calendar, map of the Tiahuanaco Empire, running tracks or weaving patterns.

One lady, Doctor Reiche from Germany, has devoted her life to studying them and has even had a platform put up at her own expense enabling some of the designs to be seen (it is her view that it is a calendar). Otherwise, the only way to see the Lines is to take a flight over them. It is no longer possible to walk or drive over them.

Crazy though it seems now, we felt at the time that we had neither the money nor the time to break our journey and see them. Peru is possibly the most interesting South American country from a historical viewpoint, and, with a little more time, a little more money and a lot less warning about the need for caution, we would have visited Cuzco to the east and explored the ancient Inca and Aztec settlements. As it was, from the minute we entered, we really only had one thing on our minds: to be through it and out again as quickly as possible.

Shortly after leaving Nazca, we saw our first Peruvian tree, and some fields, but were soon back into the sand desert. For the final few hours into Lima, the landscape was much greener, we were close to beaches to the west, and mountain ranges to the east, and trees were in abundance.

On the outskirts of Lima, a scruffy man came onto the bus, or to be more accurate, he staggered onto it. He looked around 60 and was obviously the worse for drink. He started shouting at a few

102

of the women on the bus; we could not comprehend what he said, and it may well be that we were not alone.

The women shouted at the driver and co-driver to do something, but they did nothing. Everybody else just watched, and the man remained on the bus, being generally abusive, but attracting no real reaction. So much for the supposed fiery Latin American temperament: in all our time in this reputedly volatile Continent I cannot recall, anywhere on the trip, witnessing a fight or even so much as a flash of anger or temper.

We wanted to avoid staying in central Lima. The *South American Handbook* recommended the Youth Hostel at Miraflores, Lima's largest suburb.

"It would be better to get off before the Central Station," a man on the bus informed us, "then you can take a taxi to Miraflores."

It was 8.00 pm and already dark. He came off the bus with us and hailed a taxi. Whether he had intended to leave the bus then, or whether this was the first of many displays of Peruvian generosity, we were not sure.

It was probably pushing our luck, but we had rather hoped that he would also come in the taxi with us. We had no idea how safe Lima taxi drivers were, in which direction we should be going, or what it should cost. He did at least make sure that the taxi driver knew where we wanted, and we shook hands, bidding a reluctant farewell.

Ridiculous thoughts such as, "What if the taxi driver is really a guerrilla?" crossed my mind for the next nail biting 20 minutes or so, and it was with enormous relief that we finally saw a sign proclaiming, "Miraflores Youth Hostel".

It was with much less relief, but more surprise, that the fare came to around two dollars: the risk of being ripped off had been the least of our worries, but it seemed that we had not even suffered that. Perhaps Peru is not going to be so bad after all.

Chapter 26

THE YOUTH HOSTEL was not like an English Youth Hostel where you share a bedroom and bathroom with several others, and sweep the floor or peel some potatoes to keep the price down. It was large and spacious, we had a bedroom with private bathroom and use of cooking facilities and you did not have to do a thing for it.

I was both starving and filthy. The stomach won the day, as it always must, but there was a problem; cooking facilities were all very well, but we had nothing to cook.

"Are there any shops around?" I asked the manager.
"Just out of here, left, right and there's a little store. Perhaps 100 yards away."
"And is is safe to go out?"

This clearly perplexed him and he didn't answer.

"Isn't Lima rather dangerous?"
"Oh," he laughed, "I don't think you have a problem here."

I ventured out. It dawned on me how strange my anxiety must have seemed to him: like a foreigner reading of a disturbance in central London, and asking if it is safe to walk to a corner shop in Croydon.

After a fairly lengthy session of eating, followed by an equally long time under the shower, we were fit for nothing but catching up on a lot of lost sleep.

Jo was anxious to head straight off the next day. Unless we left very early however we would reach the border at night the next day, and leaving very early did not seem a viable option. We decided to just relax in Miraflores for the day and book tickets for early the next morning.

Miraflores had attractive buildings, both brick and stone, and generally had a peaceful, attractive and affluent feel. I felt more and more stupid about asking if it was safe to go to the shop.

I chatted to some American ladies who lived in Miraflores and worked in a shop there.

"Do you think that it's safe in Lima?" I asked them.
"Miralfores is OK but Lima, no. Don't go to Lima. Certainly until after the Election.'
"We were planning to take the bus out tomorrow."

This sent them into a state of near apoplexy.

"Oh no, don't do that. You can't do that, it's not safe. There are lots of hold ups, you know."

Whether it should have done or not, I don't know, but that comment proved decisive; we decided to wait around for what was now only another four days.

I went to the American Embassy to try to find a friend of a friend of ours who apparently worked there. It seemed, however, that, if she ever had, she no longer did, as nobody knew of her. Whilst waiting, however, a conversation took place between two Americans which so struck me that I furtively wrote it down verbatim.

A young American, wearing T shirt, cut jeans and sandals, entered with what looked like a Peruvian girl. I had in fact heard him before I had seen him, a not uncommon experience with Americans. He talked to her fairly loudly, and, if she didn't appear to understand, which seemed to be most of the time, he merely repeated it, but louder.

Another American then entered, carrying two young Peruvian looking children. The one with the cut jeans approached him:

"Hi, are you from the States?"
"Yup."
"Which part?"
"Texas."
"Oh, yeah, North Carolina," (which presumably meant that that was where he came from).
"I recognise your accent, bit stronger in Texas."
"Yeah, I guess, so what's it like here? It seems kind of smoggy."
"I've been here four years, it's bad smog. It sucks."

"Tell me, how do I go about getting a work Visa for here?"

"It's kind of complex," and then the one with the children went into great detail about forms, registration, etc. He certainly made it sound complex.

As he was doing this, the one with the cut jeans suddenly exclaimed:

"Gee, take a look at that baby – God, that's a big one, ain't it?"

I looked over and saw a young Peruvian lady holding a baby, clearly blissfully ignorant of the attention now drawn to it.

The American went over to her.

"How much does that weigh?" he asked her, and seemed surprised, though nobody else was, at the lack of response. I decided that my answer to his question about the work Visa would have been to tell him to start learning some Spanish.

"God," he continued, "that must have been 20 pounds when that was born."

The other American asked the lady in Spanish and then informed his fellow countryman that in fact it was 10 pounds.

To my surprise, and I think the other American's relief, that shut him up.

I thought a lot about going to Lima. The American ladies had advised against, but others had said it should be O.K. until the afternoon, when demonstrations were likely to take place. Jo was understandably not keen, but we had to go to book the bus tickets anyway, and decided to chance it together.

You had to be quite acrobatic to catch the bus into Lima. It could not have ben more packed. There were people with one leg on and one leg off. It took 30 minutes and cost the princely sum of three pence, although if the conductor actually managed to collect it from many I would be surprised. I had some money stuffed down my pants and Jo had some down her bra. Fortunately, we had kept a small amount in more accessible positions, for otherwise we may have come to regret the extent of our caution.

We did not have to be in Lima for long to realise that the Military was in control. Armed men were on virtually every street corner; apparently there were 30,000 of them in all. They did, as the man on the bus had said they would, make me feel safer. I assumed, wrongly as it transpired, that they had the same effect on Jo. The sight of guns, sometimes pointing in our general direction, did little to ease her worries.

This misunderstanding came on top of another; I wanted to book the bus tickets before anything else and thought, wrongly, that I had communicated this fact to her. Our disagreement on the directions turned out not to be because one of us had got them wrong, but because we had both got them right, but were thinking that we were heading for different places.

These minor difficulties overcome, and the tickets booked, we began to relax and feel less on edge, seeing the armed guards more as protectors of the peace than as potential murderers.

Lima was a good deal more attractive than I expected. I had understood it to be dirty, smoggy and run-down. No doubt in parts it is, but in the heart of the city there were some wonderful old colonial buildings, light red in colour, grand and imposing, and some lovely, spacious and peaceful Plazas.

We lunched in a restaurant run by nuns, although they served in normal clothing. Our onion soup and conger eel were certainly passable, but we were to fare better elsewhere.

Generally, in Lima, we found that the best, and also by far the cheapest, food, was to be had in small back street restaurants frequented by the locals, rather than the smarter, almost glitzy, and much larger, restaurants which predominated in Miraflores and which seemed to cater more for the tourists.

Cerviche is a deservedly renowned Peruvian dish: raw white fish, seasoned with lemons, onions and red peppers, it is quite mouth watering.

Causa is less subtle in flavour but very tasty: yellow potatoes mashed with cheese, chopped ham and lemon inside, and rolled ham on top.

As in Chile, the soups were almost meals in themselves, and left me wondering again how some English eating establishments can have the ignorance and the cheek to serve from tins or packets.

Election Day was Sunday April 8th 1990. The outgoing President was President Garcia, who had served his permitted five years and was not allowed to stand again. There were several candidates, but it appeared to be a two horse race.

On the one hand, there was Vargas Llosa, a well known Peruvian writer who had come into politics relatively late; on the other, a Japanese mathematician, Alberto Fujimori, who had come into it even later and had apparently been generally unknown in Peru until only a few months before. His rating had gradually increased as Polling Day approached, and the feeling seemed to be that he might just sneak it.

The Election was taken seriously. The Peruvians had not had democracy for long and guarded it jealously. Neither propaganda nor the sale of alcohol was permitted on Election Day. It was compulsory for every Peruvian from the age of 18 to 70 to vote. One lady showed us a purple mark on her finger, and explained that it was put on when she voted and could not be removed. Presumably it could eventually, but not in time for her to have another vote.

We wandered briefly around Miraflores, and it was quiet apart from the armed military men and even tanks. If there were tanks in Miraflores, we wondered what there might be in central Lima, but our curiosity was not sufficiently strong to go and find out.

Chapter 27

WE LEFT LIMA the day after the Election, before the result was known (we found out later that it had indeed been won by Fujimori).

The bus passed the shanty towns of Northern Lima and suddenly, after about half an hour, we were into the desert; the vast ocean stretched out to our left and, to our right, sand dunes rose immediately from the road.

The road was narrow and quite bendy, the driving fast and not terribly safe. Later it levelled out and became greener, and peasants could be seen working in the fields.

After lunch, we stopped to change a wheel. Shortly afterwards, we stopped again, although we were not sure why. A little further on, we stopped again, and this time it was for real.

We were well into the desert. Nobody seemed to know what the problem was, or, if they did, they weren't telling us. After an hour or so, during which people milled around, doing nothing but not appearing to be unduly worried, a lorry arrived and our driver left in it.

"Where's he going?" we asked a fellow passenger.
"To make a phone call."
"Will he be long?"
"I think so, the nearest phone is two hours away."

There was an atmosphere of remarkable calm. It was as if this was a regular occurrence, something to which the Peruvians had become so accustomed that it did not bother them. One man, the co-driver I believe, seemed to be almost permanently flat out underneath the bus, although there did not appear to be any confidence amongst the passengers that his being there made one jot of difference to our prospects of leaving.

We thought that another bus would be the only answer. By the time the driver reached the phone, it would be 6.00 pm; it would take another bus five hours or more to arrive from Lima. The general view was that we would be lucky to be away by midnight.

If there was a saving grace, it was that we had at least stopped by a building, and, hard though it was to imagine how they could, in view of its remoteness, a few people actually lived in it.

"We can cook some fish and rice for you," they offered, "fresh fish will be delivered in a few hours."

We kept ourselves going with some bread and cucumber we had bought in Lima, and caught up with our diaries and some reading. A few hours later, we asked about the fish.

"We have missed the fish man," came the reply.

It was very difficult to see how they could have done; you could see for miles, and the arrival of the fish man must surely, we thought, be one of the highlights of the day.

One of our fellow passengers, an Ecuadorian girl, suggested that we walk to the water to try to find a fishing boat. It was only about half an hour away, across the sand dunes.

Whilst walking, we saw a new bus arrive, and rushed back. It was a false alarm; the bus was going the other way. However, it transpired that, in the meantime, the fish had arrived.

We sat with many of our fellow passengers, in what seemed to be the main room of the building, and enjoyed some tasty pieces of bass-like white fish, with suitably large quantities of rice. We were in darkness, both inside and outside the building.

Around 11.00 pm, we returned to the bus which also had no lights. What had happened to the original driver was a mystery to us all, but he had still not returned. We managed to sleep until 1.00 am, when we were awoken by a lady.

"Come out," she said to me.

I thought that another bus must have arrived, but no, at the back of the bus stood about seven men, all passengers, pushing for all their worth. I endeavoured to assist, but not a sound was coming from the engine, and it seemed to be a lost cause.

Then we tried pushing from the front, but this produced only the same stony silence from the engine. I returned to try to sleep.

Finally, at around 6.30 am, another bus arrived, and managed, presumably by jump leads although by then I was past caring how, to restore life to our engine. And so it was that, after 15 hour's standstill, and over 20 hours after departing Lima, we were finally back on the road again.

It was April 10th 1990: Jo's 26th birthday. The best that can be said for it, if anything can compensate for spending a birthday stuck in the Peruvian desert, is that it will at least be one which she is never likely to forget.

After some hours' journeying along narrow roads, through the interminable sand desert, we reached the town of Chimbote. For somewhere so far from anywhere else, its population of 185,000 seemed staggeringly high. It is Peru's largest fishing port, and, rather like Grimsby, you could smell that it was.

Out schedule, already tight, was taking a pasting; in Chimbote, we were still only 300 miles out of Lima, and 500 miles from Tumbes, the border town at which, according to the bus timetable, we should already have arrived.

We travelled the whole of that day. In the main, it was through yet more sand desert although, now and again, we passed some fields, and saw people milling around, and even a few brick shacks with bamboo roofs.

The drivers never said a word, and so we had no idea when a much needed break would next occur. When we did stop, it was at towns seemingly devoid of food shops and with loos lacking water or paper whose general aroma could almost knock you out.

It was hot and sticky on the bus. We had not showered for a few days, nor had a change of clothes. The dryness around us – the ocean was now too far away to be visible – merely exacerbated our discomfort.

After it became dark, we thought that perhaps we were now not too far from the border. We were mistaken. It was another six hours or so later when we were woken by people leaving the bus.

"Where are we?" we asked a fellow passenger sleepily. "Tumbes."

We looked at our watches. It was 2.00 am; what a time to arrive. Our fellow passengers, all clearly used to this sort of thing, and realising, which could not have been difficult, that we were not, suggested that we sleep in the streets with them.

"The first bus to the border is not until about 8.00 am. We just wait around until then."

There are three reasons why this idea did not really appeal. Firstly we had a lot more luggage to lose than they did, secondly I was desperate for a shower, and thirdly we had hardly slept for about 40 hours.

After discovering that the hotels were generally either shut or full, we finally found one which had a room.

"Do you have hot water?"

"No."

"Oh, so its only cold?"

"No."

"Pardon."

"We don't have water."

"What, no water in the whole hotel?"

"No, we don't have any."

I tried another hotel.

"Do you have water?" I asked, feeling that perhaps I should not assume that it had a bed and check that as well.

"No, not now, maybe at 8.00 am this morning."

I gave up. Jo was not so desperate for a shower, and reluctantly I joined her with our fellow passengers on the streets. They all looked fresh and cheerful, and, itchy, sticky and filthy and feeling sorry for myself though I was, it was hard not to be friendly among people who bore far worse hardships with seemingly permanent cheerfulness.

Then I became hungry. When I become hungry, I have to eat immediately or am liable to feel very faint and dizzy. Given that it was 3.00 am, this was going to be a problem. I wandered alone round the town, stomach rumbling painfully, and finally found a street vendor selling milk in a carton. It was long life, something I cannot abide, but it was that or nothing. When I opened the carton it resembled dirty water with little white flakes in it. I complained: the vendor gave me another one; it was almost as bad.

Thinking that maybe Peruvian long life looked like that, but was safe to drink, I took it back to the group. They all made it fairly clear that Peruvian long life does not look like that and that it was not safe.

I took it back. The vendor shook it, which made it a little whiter, but surely no less harmful.

"It's not safe to drink, I want my money back."

"No, it's OK."

"If it's OK, you drink it."

She put it to her mouth, but would not drink it. My money was returned.

I had to make do with some warm water from another street stall, and made a coffee, which prevented a collapse, but would hardly give me the stamina and patience likely to be needed for the task of negotiating a Peruvian Border Control.

Then I needed a loo. I went to a hotel and asked if I could use theirs but they refused.

"Why?"

"We have no water."

"Where's the loo?"

I was directed round the corner. There was no loo there, but a man was peeing in the street. I concluded that this must be a generally acceptable street to use, and joined him.

It was beginning to become light, and the day's activities seemed to be commencing, although it was only around 5.00 am. I saw a few young men drinking beer in a bar. Typically it was a small, basic and very dirty bar plagued with mosquitoes. Stalls were opening selling soft drinks, biscuits and watery juices, but not the food of substance which I craved.

A man in his sixties, wearing filthy jeans full of holes, and a T shirt and with a plastic bag on his head, passed by and muttered a few incoherent words to us. The town nutter, perhaps.

Then, suddenly, at around 5.30, whilst lying on a bench with Jo, we were stirred by others in the group.

"Vamos," they were shouting. ("Let's go.")

We followed them onto a bus, trusting them that it was heading to the border. An hour later, much further than we had assumed as people had referred to Tumbes as "the border town", we reached the border itself at what was literally the border town of Agua Verdes.

Agua Verdes was a most peculiar place: it seemed to be no more than a collection of street stalls and small shops, and the structures of thin planks of wood or bamboo had a decidedly temporary appearance. It looked as if the whole town could be blown away by a strong gust of wind.

We waited for a long time in the bus, joined a chaotic queue for the necessary exit stamp, and finally reached the border just before 9.00 am, when it was due to open.

The Peruvian–Ecuadorian border was marked by a disgustingly dirty river, the bridge over it being about 50 metres long. On either side of the bridge, a chain prevented anyone crossing outside permitted hours. There were perhaps 100 people on either side waiting quietly and patiently.

Some music played: apparently it was the countries' National Anthems. They were listened to in near silence and the chains were then removed. We walked over the river and into Ecuador. It was the first country on the trip which we had walked into.

Eight days after entering Peru in a taxi, full of fear and with reluctance, we had left it behind us, on foot, full of relief and with enormous enthusiasm. Ecuador, we had been led to believe, would be a whole different ball game.

Chapter 28

OUR SPIRITS LIFTED on entering Ecuador. We were eagerly awaiting it for three reasons in particular.

Firstly, in comparison to Peru, it would, we were led to believe, be relaxed and safe; secondly, Quito is rated as one of the continent's most attractive capitals; and thirdly, a great deal of Ecuador is jungle, and, after an overdose of Argentinian, Chilean and Peruvian desert, this would be, we anticipated, like a breath of fresh air.

The border town of Huayaquil proved to be anything but a breath of fresh air. We joined a lengthy jostling queue at the Immigration Office, and found ourselves nearly permanently harangued by slick, devious looking money changers, flashing wads of dollars and sucres in front of our faces.

Jo had managed a quick wash at Agua Verdes, but I had not, and it was now around 50 hours since I had last splashed water on my face, and had a change of clothes. After two solid days on a cramped airless bus, sweating for much of it in the heat of the desert, I was sure that my clothes would now stand up on their own; there must surely be some doubt, I thought, as to whether assistance would be required to prise them off.

Whilst Jo remained queuing, I went in search of a wash room. The first stop was a hotel.

"Do you have washing facilities?"
"No, no water."

A restaurant gave the same response. I could not believe it, and paced frantically about the town in an attempt to stop my now desperate and almost permanent need to itch.

My heart lifted on seeing a sign: "Bano Y Duchas" (bathroom and showers) but it was not to be – the door was locked. People shrugged their shoulders and smiled as I pleaded with them for water.

"No hay agua," they kept repeating (there is no water).

"For the whole day?" I asked.

"Yes, no water all day," they confirmed, in a manner so casual as to suggest that in Huayaquil water was considered to be a rare luxury.

Never before had I come across a town which not only was devoid of water but which apparently had no expectation of having any in the foreseeable future.

Rather like the traveller I was told about in China, who, frustrated by her inability to be understood, went into the middle of a street and screamed at the top of her voice: "Does anyone in this town speak English?" I had a burning desire to shout at the top of my voice: "Does this town have water?"

In some ways, I regret not having done it, but my knowledge of Ecuador's Public Order legislation, and, more importantly, of the practical Police powers and the quality of Ecuadorian prisons, was far too sketchy to take the chance.

A money changer approached us, offering 16,000 sucres for 20 dollars. We accepted, and were about to hand our 20 dollar note to him when he said, "I don't have any sucres. Give me five minutes."

In 15 minutes in Ecuador, we had not only found a town with no water but a money changer with no money. We never saw him again.

The bus to Quito would take around 13 hours, and leave in an hour. The thought of a further full day on a bus in the same clothes and still unwashed filled me with horror and anguish. I was now having to itch myself so much that to onlookers (of which there were hopefully not many) it must have appeared indecent.

In a last, desperate move, I walked stiffly and awkwardly round town, in pursuit of even a drop of elusive water. Finally, I spotted a huge container with a few gallons of it outside somebody's home. There was a young boy nearby who said I could use a bit. Whether he had authority to say so, I had no idea, but cared even less.

"Is there a bath or anywhere private?" I asked, strongly suspecting that this was looking a gift horse in the mouth.

"Try the hotel upstairs," he replied helpfully.

The hotel was run-down, its walls all bare. I explained that I had some water, and just wanted somewhere private to throw it over myself.

An obliging young man pointed to the bathroom, and, presumably out of habit, I turned the shower tap, and wonder of wonders, it worked!

Never has a shower felt so wonderful. I felt the dirt and sweat and grime literally falling off me, although some vigour was required to eject it from my hair.

I could have stayed there for hours, but this would surely deprive others, and anyway we had a bus to catch and Jo would be wondering where I was.

Walking back in a fresh T shirt and shorts, I felt like a new man, rejuvenated and lighter. Instead of dreading it, I now awaited the bus journey with relish.

Chapter 29

HOW DIFFERENT the Ecuadorian bus was to any we had seen so far! A kaleidoscope of bright colours on the outside, light and airy inside, it had a roof so low that even we had to stoop slightly, small metal luggage holders above us and seats with plastic covers on them.

While it had none of the luxuries to which, Peru excepting, we had become accustomed – bathroom facilities, curtains, videos, plenty of legroom, another compartment for luggage – it was the first that could be said to have any real character and to provide a sense of excitement.

The landscape was in the main flat and certainly not spectacular, but the sight of grass and trees after such a prolonged absence lifted our hearts. It was not just the occasional field and the occasional tree either; for the first few hours of the journey, we saw little else. Banana plantations lined both sides of the road almost continuously. It came as no surprise to learn that Ecuador is the world's largest banana exporter.

The desert which had so dominated our travels since leaving Santiago now seemed a million miles away rather than the 50 or so that it actually was. I cannot ever recall experiencing such a sudden and complete transformation of landscape on crossing a border. We were in no doubt that it was a change very much for the better.

We stopped quite frequently on the roadside to have our passports checked. This was, we were told, on account of the problem of terrorism, although nobody suggested that it was anything to worry about.

In Machala, where we stopped for lunch, a Banana Fair is held every September. Given that the road to it was dominated by them, bananas were surprisingly conspicuous by their absence in the town itself.

Lunch consisted of chicken, noodle and coriander soup and a quite delicious drink called "Mora" which seemed to comprise blackberries and milk. More Mora was offered on the bus, along with water melons, fritters and pieces of coconut; bananas were again sadly absent.

The afternoon's journey was more of the same; banana plantations all the way, interspersed with the occasional coconut tree, and less occasional flimsy property comprising planks of wood, corrugated iron and bamboo.

From the moment we stepped out of our spacious two pounds per night hotel the next morning, Quito struck as a very special city. We were in the Old City. Its streets were narrow, its buildings white and elegant with little blue balconies, its shops small and individual. Ladies sat in the street selling apples from a basket. Lush green hills rose steeply in the near distance.

Probably on account mainly of the hills, it reminded me a little of Bath, which surely has one of the finest settings of any English city. It came as no surprise to learn that Quito stands at 2,850 metres: only one South American city is higher, the Bolivian Capital, La Paz, which is the highest in the world.

It was a Welsh playboy, Beau Nash, in search of an English playground, who had fallen in love with the setting of Bath in the early 18th century, and had decided to develop a city to match it. Quito had likewise been selected on account of its surrounding landscape, albeit a few centuries earlier. Quito's "Beau Nash" were the Incas from Peru, whose scarch for a settlement in the north of the continent ended when they spotted the hollow that is now Quito.

We visited a miniature model of the old colonial town of Quito.

"It took me six years to construct it," the model's maker informed us. "It is very sad," he continued, "but when the Spaniards arrived in the 19th century, they took much of the gold, and rebuilt the city largely on top of the old Inca city."

It was Holy Week. On Good Friday, April 13th, an enormous procession took place through the old city of Quito. It seemed to have the sort of following which in England would be reserved for

Royal Weddings or bus top parades of a triumphant football team, Cup in hand.

The participants were in the main dressed in purple; some even sported a purple cone which rose several feet above their head. Many wore masks which, apart from small slits to enable them to see and to breathe, covered their entire face; some carried a cross.

People lined the streets as far as the eye could see, jostling for position. It was, however, an orderly and well behaved crowd. Despite the proximity to each other, some Indian ladies were breast feeding their babies, an act which would probably have caused some consternation at a Royal Wedding or even at the parade of a football team, but which in Quito seemed to cause nobody, ourselves excepting (and we soon became used to it), to bat an eyelid.

Those who were fortunate enough to have them, or perhaps to know people who had them, enjoyed a bird's eye view from the balconies which so many of Old Quito's properties possessed.

The strength of Catholicism was also evident in Quito's churches. The city has 86 in all, although we visited only a handful. In one, the crypt was just a mass of gold, one that the Spanish had missed perhaps. In another lay a model of Jesus, covered in blood. People were touching his feet with cotton wool. A few of them were extremely old ladies with an air of dogged determination; many looked to be only in their twenties.

If one thing could be said to have been a disappointment in Old Quito, it was the food. Not only was it bland and tasteless, but there seemed to be little variety and it was also relatively expensive – perhaps as much as three pounds for a meal.

Everywhere seemed to offer the same standard menu of chicken or fish or meat with rice. Much was made of the special Holy Week soup called Fanecsa, a rich soup based on salty fish, pieces of meat and beans, but sadly this too had a bland flavour.

Coffee was generally Chilean style; a cup of boiled water and a jar of instant plonked on the table and you were left to get on with it. At least, however, Quito heralded a long-awaited return to fresh milk, and the Mora continued to be wonderful.

Food apart, we had enjoyed our few days in Quito; next stop was Otavalo Market in the north, followed by an eagerly awaited visit to the Ecuadorian Jungle.

Chapter 30

OTAVALO IS A TWO HOUR bus journey north of Quito along windy roads passing through a dramatic landscape of deep valleys. The *South American Handbook* describes it as "a must for tourists". We could not say that we had not been warned.

At the risk of generalisation, a tourist is different to a traveller. A tourist is likely to be on holiday, perhaps on a package tour, wants everything organised by somebody else and insists on the creature comforts. A tourist is generally more interested in sights than in the people of the country.

A traveller, on the other hand, wants to see what a country and its people are really like. A traveller will have nothing pre-arranged, making all the decisions and booking all journeys and accommodation on the spur of the moment. A traveller may not necessarily despise creature comforts, but is prepared to sacrifice them so as to travel for longer on limited funds. A traveller may on average be 20 to 30 years younger than a tourist, and may have the same sort of money for six months that the tourist will have for two weeks.

This difference (and I do stress that it is not true in all cases) is, I think, generally acknowledged, and is not intended in any way to give offence. I have already explained that travellers can, by their obsessions with bargains and cost cutting, give a very bad impression to locals.

Nonetheless, there are places where tourism could be said to have left an indelible, and not necessarily agreeable, mark. Otavalo struck us as such a place.

The market is rated primarily for its woollens; from ponchos to bobble hats, rugs to socks and gloves to jumpers. The first striking thing about it was its sheer size: 100 or more stalls crammed into the Market Square. This "en masse" type selling rather put us off from the outset; when you can see so many of a particular item, being sold by so many people in close proximity, it is hard to have the feeling that you are buying something special.

The Indian vendors seemed pushy, and some sneered at you if, having spent even a brief period looking at their wares, you then moved on without buying. Bargaining was expected, but it was not fun in the way that bargaining can be. It was an aggressive, competitive sort of bargaining, without humour or feeling. We bargained a rug down from 5,500 sucres to 4,000 sucres (about £3) and our vendor handed it to us with no apparent sign of pleasure at providing something which we were happy to have purchased, and for a sum which many Ecuadorians would not earn in a day.

In short, there was a tension in the air between the locals and the foreigners. They wanted our money; we wanted their products. The sad thing was that that was all it seemed to be about. Neither seemed interested in the other; it was a market devoid of soul.

We returned to Quito for a night, and spent the next day on a bus travelling south east to Mishuali. Although a distance of only some 200 miles, the roads were such that it took around nine hours to cover it.

"It is tranquil here in Ecuador," our driver told us, "We have no serious problems. Our Government is OK, but there are not enough jobs. We have some in bananas, in oil and a few in coffee, rice and dairy farming, but many people don't have work."

In the afternoon, it poured with rain (a not uncommon occurrence during our time in Ecuador), and the narrow, muddy track which was our route was barely passable. If visibility had been any less, I doubt if the driver could have continued.

Mishuali is all wooden and bamboo huts with thatched roofs. Arriving there and strolling around was like going back in time. Everywhere had signs advertising "Jungle Tours"; all seemed to be claiming that their's was the best.

We found a wonderful residencia on the main square, where our bedroom appeared to have been constructed almost entirely out of tree trunks, and went in search of what really would be "the best Jungle tour".

One young local told us he had good contacts with the Indians living in the Jungle, and, keen as we were to have at least an insight into the lives they lead, he was in the reckoning.

However, he spoke no English, and as our technical Spanish was poor, this factor ultimately led us to discard him. We were subsequently to discover that he prepares all his own food from the Jungle and so you end up eating monkeys and the like, and thought then that his lack of English had turned out to be a blessing in disguise.

We eventually settled for a guide by the name of Pepe whose English was good and with whom, along with four others, we would spend three days, based at a purpose-built "Jungle campsite".

When Jo and I had first discussed the detail of the trip, which was probably only a few months before it started, I recall how excited she had been about the prospect of visiting the Jungle. We were very contented that night as we fell asleep to the smell of the surrounding tree trunks.

Chapter 31

THE DAY STARTED with bread and jam, scrambled eggs and coffee (in that order, strangely), and we then walked the short distance to the river. Two monkeys were swinging and hanging precariously from trees, performing acrobatics that would have graced any Olympic Gymnastics Team.

We crossed the river by canoe, and could see the local Indians squatting on the edge in pursuit of gold.

"They work from 6.00 am to 6.00 pm every day," Pepe told us, "and collect perhaps a few ounces which they then sell in Mishuali."

Any illusions we may have had about life in the Jungle being one long holiday were instantly shattered. This was excruciatingly boring and back-breaking work, undertaken, it seemed, for most of the hours of daylight.

Pepe hit a rubber tree with a knife, and milk emerged, running down the tree. I stopped some with a finger and tasted it: very creamy, and certainly acceptable. Give me rubber tree milk over long life any day.

I took some more on another finger, but this time did not lick it. Very quickly the milk coagulated into what we think of as rubber. So the Jungle inhabitants have not only an instant source of nutrition but also something which they can use like string.

There were also some elephant plants imported from Africa. They are light green, tall, thin and poisonous. The Indians attach such plants to a piece of wood, one end of which they have cut into a sharp point, and fire it out of a four metre long blow pipe. It can apparently travel 40 metres, and the idea is to strike it at monkeys from such a distance that they cannot see you. The poison takes about a minute to take effect, and the monkey then drops off the tree, dead.

Another tree, Pepe informed us, contains a substance which is used by the ladies of the jungle as a contraceptive pill. Given that males outnumber females by seven to one, it seemed that this tree was perhaps the most important in the whole Jungle. Unfortunately however it was not entirely reliable, and girls as young as 14 have become pregnant.

We never walked far without coming across further examples of the Jungle's natural provision for its inhabitants' needs. Apparently, deeper into the jungle you see deer, boars, parrots and monkeys. We did not, and the swarm of ants, a few frogs and two cows were a pretty mediocre substitute.

We finally reached "base camp" late that afternoon, having walked through what was mainly primary, though sometimes secondary, jungle. "Base camp" had been purpose-built out of trees and leaves. Accommodation was a small square hut on stilts of tree trunks, with an enormous and essential mosquito net covering the bed.

After a swim in the River Napo (a tributary of the Amazon, which was some 300 miles to the east), we sat in the shade for lunch. During the course of it, I felt something against my leg: closer inspection revealed, initially to my horror, that it was a wild boar, its brittle hairs against my bare leg. The shock wore off speedily and the boar proved to be quite friendly.

The same could not be said for our next companion: an ant eater. It most closely resembles a cat although with a much longer mouth, and it can not only get you with its claws but with its teeth as well. I was far more wary of it than of the boar.

The rest of that day was pleasantly lazy and peaceful. Camp was literally on the bank of the river, and, as it was around 100° during the day, we took frequent dips, to swim, canoe, or float along on rubber tyres, carried, sometimes at a fair speed, by the current.

When not in the water, we lay on a hammock and listened (or at least heard) as the American in the group provided his life history (something Americans seem fond of doing) and, after supper, broke into song and played the guitar.

The next day, we embarked on another walk, and Pepe demonstrated the animal traps. The ones we saw were for tourists' eyes only, the proper ones being much deeper into the jungle, but they seemed authentic enough. One caused a heavy plank of wood to fall and crush the animal; another strangled birds and another caused a door to shut when an animal enters leaving it trapped but still alive. This is a typical chicken trap and avoids the risk of damaging the skin.

The cruelest trap, it seemed to me, was one designed to catch deer and boars. A hole is dug, and pieces of thin, sharpened wood are put vertically into it, sharp end pointing upwards. Leaves then cover the top of the hole, and animals treading on the leaves drop onto the points.

I once read the story of the American Jim Thompson who developed the Thai silk industry after the Second World War and who mysteriously disappeared in the Malaysian Jungle. His body has never been found, and one possibility is that he fell down a trap set for animals and that even an extensive search could not detect all such traps. It would, however, have had to have been a considerably larger trap than this one.

It was not until the last day, stopping off on the river bank whilst returning to Mishuali, by canoe, that we finally came across some of the people for whom the jungle is home. The village had a population of approximately 700, two schools, one primary and the other missionary, and a few small and very basic shops. It was primarily an Indian village; the whites kept together in one part of it, and neither apparently liked to mix with the other.

The houses were mainly constructed from palm and bamboo; the newer ones, however, had corrugated iron roofs. This created a tension: the older generation liked self-sufficiency; the new did not mind importing into the jungle what it saw as better quality material.

The few Indians that we saw were just sitting around, some playing cards, and gave us a fairly frosty reception. Rather like the Australian Aborigines, it did not seem that they liked tourists, or at least the idea that they were somehow "on show". I recall seeing a sign in the Australian outback around Ayers Rock, which said: "Please do not photograph Aborigines. We are not animals at a zoo." It would not have surprised me to see a similar sign from the Indians here.

"What do these Indians do?" we asked Pepe.

"Mainly they try to find gold, they hunt, do a bit of farming and make a few artesan goods, for example with the feathers of the birds they trap. On the whole they are reasonably civilised, the children go to school up to at least the age of 12 years, quite often travelling by canoe."

Pepe told us, also, that there is one uncivilised tribe deep in the jungle who a few years before had killed two missionaries, one a Spanish man and the other a Colombian lady. They stabbed them with poisonous spears and their bodies revealed around 100 wounds. It was reminiscent of the contempt held by the Indians in Tierra del Fuego for the English missionaries over 100 years earlier.

The final part of the journey back to Mishuali was hazardous to say the least. There were about seven of us in the canoe. Suddenly the heavens opened. We put a plastic cover over us, but this had to be held up and made it difficult for us to see. The canoe was gradually becoming waterlogged and toppled a lot from side to side. It seemed only a matter of time before it toppled right over, but, as suddenly as it started, the rain stopped again, and we made it back safely.

It had been an interesting and fun three days: the right balance of walking, canoeing, relaxing and talking. I had found the lack of food a problem, and we had both suffered from mosquito bites, but these were small sacrifices. Having gone backwards to do this trip, we were now in urgent need of making some progress. It was 19th April 1990. We had less than six weeks to reach Vancouver, and were not quite half way on the 12,000 mile journey from the bottom of the world. Any further backward move was out of the question.

Chapter 32

RETURNING TO OUR HOTEL in Quito felt like returning home. The owners treated us like long-lost friends, and we appreciated its space and the sense of security and comfort it gave us. This feeling was probably exacerbated by a sense of considerable anxiety about our future movements.

The next two countries, heading north, are Colombia and Panama. Neither could be said to be likely to invoke a sense of well-being, and the thought of the two in rapid succession was like a double dose of terror.

Obtaining information in Quito was a challenge in itself. We needed to know whether we could enter Colombia without having a ticket to leave it. The *South American Handbook* said that we could not; the Colombian Embassy in Quito did not know, nor did it have any information about booking tickets or indeed seemingly about anything at all.

We took a taxi into "downtown" or "New" Quito. It was much like any large "downtown": lots of high-rise buildings, hotels, banks, and most importantly for us, airline offices. We finally tracked down the office of "Avianca", the Colombian airline, and explained what we wanted.

"You must buy a ticket here to leave Colombia. But also you must buy a ticket to leave Panama. They won't let you into Panama without a ticket out."

We knew that the only way to travel from Colombia to Panama was by air; determined though we were to do the whole trip over land, this part, and this part alone, was impossible – there are simply no road or rail links between the two countries. However we also knew that we wanted to travel overland out of Panama.

"We don't want to fly out of Panama."

"Then you can cancel that flight once in Panama, provided you produce a bus ticket in its place."

It sounded logical enough, but it also sounded decidedly iffy. The trouble was that we could not find the Panamanian Embassy in Quito, nor was there any other sure way we could think of to check it out. Time did not allow us to delay.

We took the bull by the horns and booked two tickets: Cali – Panama – Sane Jose, Costa Rica. They cost around £150 each, a large chunk out of our budget but unavoidable, and about £50 each, according to the theory, would be recovered. Given that there is no alternative but to fly, it is hardly surprising that the Colombia to Panama flight, a journey of around one hour, is grossly over priced.

The flight was at lunch time in two day's time. We woke at 3.30 the next morning for an early bus out of Quito. After the all too common problem on Ecuadorian buses of other people being on our seats and refusing to budge was resolved when the people in them eventually realised that they were on the wrong bus, we were on our way.

It was a lovely journey north, through lush green scenery alongside many dramatically steep hills and passing a few volcanoes. There were more Indians walking along the road than cars on it. After only about four hours, we reached the border town of Tulcan.

There were supposed to be buses to the border itself but we couldn't find them, and took a taxi instead. Just as our entry into Ecuador had been on foot, so too was the exit from it, the border again being marked by a river. Our Exit visas had been stamped in a matter of minutes, and to our surprise it was almost as easy on the Colombian side.

There was the usual gathering of sleazy looking money changers carrying wads of notes and pocket calculators. We were only going to be in Colombia for around 30 hours and obtained 460 Colombian pesos for 40 dollars in the hope that it would last us. A bus that was really more like a wagon, with torn seats and a capacity of eight, transported us to the centre of our first Colombian town. Ipiales seemed most attractive: there were plazas and a lot of properties with balconies, and horses and carts outnumbered motor vehicles.

People had not warned us off Colombia in the way that they had warned us off Peru. Thieving was certainly considered a problem, but the general view seemed to be that it was mainly confined to the larger cities. Unless stupid enough to become involved, the drugs problem was not one that should cause travellers any loss of sleep. Having said that, news of the recent murder of seven people in Cali, to which we were heading, hardly inspired confidence.

I can say without hesitation that I have never witnessed scenery as dramatic as that on the journey from Ipiales to Popayan. We had been given a hint of it by Paul Theroux's description of a train journey in this part of Colombia in *The Old Patagonian Express*, but it had to be seen to be believed.

We were travelling through the Cordillera, supposedly a more inhabited region of Colombia, although it was hard to believe it; we hardly saw a building or person for hours. The road was just a succession of sharp bends, rising steeply, and weaved us around a range of brown-green mountains which stretched as far as the eye could see.

The valleys were deep; often they were river valleys with a little vegetation and even a few small trees, fir trees I believe, at the foot. Sometimes there was a sheer drop from the roadside of several hundred yards. One mistake by our driver (or indeed another road user although there were fortunately very few of them) and we would all just have been statistics. The bus at the bottom of the valley would, I imagine, have been barely visible from the top. I do not think that we took our eyes of the road for several hours, partly out of wonderment, partly out of fear.

We decided to stay in Popayan and take an early bus to Cali the next day, as, from all accounts, Popayan was considerably safer. Nonetheless the lady in whose house we stayed still advised us that it was too dangerous to go out at night: "Too many robbers, tourists should not be on the streets after dark," she informed us. It was advice which we reluctantly accepted.

We were somewhat anxious about going to Cali, not just because of its reputation but also because we were not convinced

130

that the flight would actually materialise. We need not have been. The three hour bus journey took us straight to the airport, and, after an understandably thorough, but very friendly, security check, we not only had our tickets confirmed, but also had it confirmed again that the Panama to San Jose flight could be cashed in in Panama.

Our final meal in Colombia of chicken, greasy chips, salad and coffee was more reminiscent of Gatwick Airport or even Joe's Cafe than Cali Airport, but this was the last thing on our minds. We had gone to Colombia because it was the next country on the way north rather than for culinary or indeed any other experience. Colombian food may have passed us by, but the scenery of the Cordillera will be something we will never forget.

Chapter 33

THE AMERICAN'S DRAMATIC SEIZURE of General Noriega had taken place only four months previously. We wondered as we touched down in Panama City whether we might be confused for Americans and therefore be at risk.

If the reaction we received at the airport was anything to go by, we would not have a problem. After all the fuss about a ticket out being essential, the smiling customs officer did not even require to see it. To our query as to whether it was safe to take a bus into the centre, a smiling lady at the airline informed us that if we had survived Colombia, we should be OK here.

The bus was a mass of blue, purple, green and yellow both inside and outside, had a blow horn the like of which I had not seen for years and blaring music. We soon realised that there was nothing unusual or coincidental about the smiling customs officer and the smiling airline assistant. Everybody who embarked on the bus did so with a smile. They were almost all West Indians. One, standing at the front, welcomed everyone aboard, even though it appeared to us that he was a passenger himself. If only travelling on English buses was this much fun, we thought.

After 45 minutes of music, smiling and laughter, we were in the New City. One passenger directed us towards the pensioni that we were seeking, and as we neared it, we were inundated with others seemingly eager to help: "Hey man, where you wanting? Let me show you, man." The final chap walked us to the door.

Apart from being struck by the friendliness of the people and the fact that they generally seemed to speak English, we were also struck by the oppressive heat – it seemed airless and heavy and we were dripping with sweat having carried our luggage about a mile. The pensioni was in a run-down area in an older part of the city.

It was very cramped and washing seemed to hang from virtually every balcony. There were a lot of blacks milling around. One had his fists clenched and was doing what appeared to be Kung Fu movements at nobody in particular. We gave him the benefit of the doubt, deciding that he may well be drunk.

All in all, it was not a very pleasant area to wander around, and so we went for a meal in the first place we saw. It was appalling. We felt as if we were in an institution. The food sat uninvitingly in trays above which was the description of it (generally necessary) and its price (excessive). The food was little short of American-style fast food. You had to queue for it, and give your orders to "dinner ladies" and then you had to sit at a food counter on a round chair and plough you way through it.

My ham omelette and rice with a sweet brown sauce was repulsive and I felt relieved that I was not too hungry. Jo had meat, rice and salad and, to say the least, did not enjoy them. Few things get my back up more than having a bad meal, and Jo, whose sense of taste is finely tuned, is of the same ilk. It was a most depressing experience.

The atmosphere was not helped by the "dinner ladies" telling us how dangerous the area is.

"You must take a taxi back," they insisted.

"But we're only five blocks away," we replied.

"It doesn't matter. It's dangerous. They'll rob you," countered the ladies making a stabbing action as if to reinforce the point.

Another girl, also black, nodded in approval and then the two dinner ladies smiled and said together, "It's dangerous."

The whole thing looked so synchronised that we wondered if this was a little routine they went through whenever they saw a foreigner. And then, to cap it all, a man entered, came over to us and said quietly; "Be careful – it's very dangerous here," smiling as he said it.

We walked back to the pensioni, not without hesitation and not without keeping our wits about us, and were not robbed once. Later that night in the pensioni we overheard a conversation about where in the city is dangerous, where's safe, and where's a bit in the middle. It was obvious that danger was a popular topic of conversation for the inhabitants of Panama City.

It seems to me to be a good idea, when travelling one step at a time as we were, to make arrangements to leave a place as soon as possible after arriving. It avoids the risk of leaving it to the day you want to leave only to discover that there's no way out for another week. It also enables you to relax in the knowledge that what must be done has been done (a state of affairs I find is not limited only to travelling). Whilst it removes the flexibility as to how long you will stay, this flexibility was in our case all but removed anyway by the demands of our time scale.

In Panama, we had even more reason to make this our first priority; a niggling suspicion that the exchange of plane for bus tickets would not be as smooth as the ladies in the airline office in Quito had assured us it would be. It was. We acquired bus tickets not only from Panama to San Jose, Costa Rica but also on from San Jose to Managua, Nicaragua, a total distance of some 900 miles, traded in the flight tickets and made a healthy profit.

We did very little for the rest of that first day; for the first time on the trip we both felt lousy. It may have been the food or it may have been the climate. It was stifling during the day, cooling noticeably after about five o'clock and then before seven o'clock it was dark.

Wandering back to our pensioni, we were struck by the rubbish piled up on every street corner, by the dilapidated state of the buildings and by the fact that people's front doors seemed to be left open, revealing the contents of their front rooms: typically a collection of family photographs, statues of Christ and people watching television.

Tomorrow, we hoped, would be better. We would go early to a Yacht Club and offer our services as linehandlers in the hope of making a journey through the Panama Canal.

Chapter 34

OUR TAXI DRIVER descended, as so many Panamanians do, from British West Indians brought into Panama in the second half of the 19th century to build first the railway and then the canal.

The British West Indians in Panama spoke perfect English, as well of course as Spanish, but their accent and speed made them very difficult to understand. Indeed, on one occasion, not being able to comprehend a word that one had said, I asked him to speak English, only to discover that he had been. Fortunately, this taxi driver, whilst requiring concentration, was not quite that bad.

"How long have you been in Panama?"

"Aah born here."

"Do you like it?"

"Sure, it's my country. It's better after de invasion."

"You supported the invasion?"

"Sure, everybody did. He was a bad man dat Noriega. Aah don't know what's goin' a happen to him now."

We arrived at the entrance to a Military Base and were greeted by a young uniformed American soldier.

"Who are you?" he asked aggressively. He was clearly not a man who believed in wasting words.

"We're English, waiting to visit the Balbao Yacht Club."

"Got any ID?"

"I'm just de taxi driver, man," replied the taxi driver even though the question had been directed at us.

We handed him copies of our passports.

"Just a minute, wait outside," and the soldier went off; we were not quite sure why.

Our driver explained that this had been joint United States–Panamanian territory but since the invasion it belonged only to the U.S., and security had obviously tightened. The soldier returned.

"I've just called my boss. I need your passport, not a copy."

"But we don't carry our passports on us in case they get stolen."

He went off to call his boss again.

"O.K., my boss says you can go in, but not the taxi."

Since it was only a five minute walk through the Base to the Yacht Club, this was not a problem.

An American was standing outside the bar. He had sailed from Acapulco in seven days, had arrived at 4.00 am and was desperate for the bar to open. There were several West Indians around. One told us that the bar would open at 11.00, another said 11.30. The American had been told 10.30. In the end, nobody could find the key so it didn't open at all. Although I did not realise it at the time, this was a good early indication of the way in which Panama operated.

We never did manage to take a trip through the canal, simply not managing to be in the right place at the right time. We did however visit several sections of it, saw ships being guided through the locks and learnt much both of its history and its operation.

The Panama Canal is one of the two most strategic artificial waterways in the world, the other of course being the Suez.

Its importance cannot be underestimated; it is the only passageway throughout the entire continent of America enabling ships to travel between the Atlantic and the Pacific Ocean. The saving in time is immense. For example, a boat travelling from the West coast of the United States to the East coast of the United States which took the only alternative route, going round the Southern tip of Argentina, would travel some 8,000 nautical miles further than one using the Panama Canal.

You only have to look at a map of the continent to see why Panama was the obvious site for an Atlantic to Pacific canal: it is quite simply, at 40 miles, the shortest distance by far between the two Oceans.

The Americans had first made use of Panama's strategic position by constructing (or rather by importing British West

Indians to construct) a railway line linking the Atlantic and the Pacific. At the time it was finished (1853) there was no rail road across the United States and the line proved invaluable.

It was not the Americans, however, but the French, who initially set about the task of constructing the canal. A Frenchman by the name of Ferdinand de Lesseps, who had supervised the building of the Suez Canal, arrived in Panama in around 1880, set up a company to construct the canal and put thousands upon thousands of workers to the task.

Some 10 years and 20 miles of canal later, the company crashed. Whilst poor planning and fraud have been blamed, it appears that the primary cause of the downfall was malaria. During that 10 year period, approximately 22,000 workers died.

At that time, Panama was still only a Department of Colombia and the Colombian Senate refused to agree to the transfer of the canal-building rights and properties to the United States. Panama eventually declared its independence in 1903, and by a treaty of the same year, the United Sates was given the sole right to control and operate the Canal Zone.

According to a French-Panamanian whom we met, the Americans were fortunate. In the intervening period between the French company's collapse and the Americans starting work, the Cuban, Dr Finlay, had discovered a means of preventing malaria. Had he done so earlier, we were told, it would be the French, and not the Americans, who controlled the canal. It sounded plausible enough, although it is a claim I have never seen or heard anywhere else.

There is no doubt however that a great deal of thought and skill went into the eventual building of the canal, and after about 10 years of hard work, the first ship was able to pass through it, on August 15th 1914.

The biggest decision for the Americans had been whether to build a sea-level canal or a lake – and – lock canal. Had the land been flat, the former would no doubt have been much easier, but it was not. Although, as luck would have it, there was a natural gap between the high mountain ranges to the west and those to the east of Panama City, there were still fluctuations in the height of the land along the canal's intended route.

It was considered at that time that the answer was to have locks to bring the ships up and down to the natural lie of the land. Several locks were constructed, and at one, Gatun Locks, a series of three locks lifts ships a total of 85 feet.

Such is the narrowness of the locks that, small vessels apart, all ships have to be towed through by towing locomotives. Tracks run alongside the locks, and the locomotives move along them at a speed of two miles per hour pulling the ship forward whilst at the same time keeping it steady and in line. Each ship normally requires six locomotives. It is possible, and indeed quite common, for ships going in different directions to each other to be passing through a lock at the same time.

It is generally considered that a ship should take around 24 hours to pass through the canal. There is no problem about continuing through the night: lights and buoys ensure that it can be negotiated safely.

Politically, the canal is changing. Although the United States had been given the Canal Zone in 1903 for time immemorial, the Panamanians later sought to renege on the agreement, and indeed the United States acquiesced. By the Panama Canal Treaty of 1978, it was agreed that Panama would acquire increased responsibilities for the canal, and that from the year 2000 it would be in Panama's complete control.

How will this affect the operation of the canal? From what we gleaned, admittedly during a stay of only four days, it could well be a disaster.

The Panamanians already have control of the railway which runs, more or less, parallel to the canal. We rose early one morning to catch the 6.45 am train north out of Panama City, having checked the timetable the previous day. Not only was there no sign of a train but there was no sign of any official either. A few people told us, casually, that it should arrive soon.

Then an official ambled onto the platform.

"When's the train arriving?"

"Der's no train between December and June," the official replied, smiling.

"But the timetable says there's one at 6.45."

"Yes, but der isn't."

"Can you put a sign up saying there isn't?"

He smiled again, and gave a look which suggested that he couldn't see what the problem was.

"O.K.," he replied, without conviction.

"Can you do it now?"

"No, later, I can't get into de office now."

The idea of doing something now seemed to be alien to the Panamanians; indeed I sometimes wondered if doing something at any time was.

We found out later that the track was so overgrown with grass that the train either simply could not get through or alternatively would be derailed. Some people doubted whether it would ever run again.

One of the canal workers we talked to was an American.

"I fought in Vietnam for 13½ months, then I was looking for something to do and didn't want to go back to the States so I came here. I've been here 23 years. This was the place to be. We had everything. It was all cheap," and then he paused and looked as if he wanted to say much more, but simply finished:

"It's not how it was."

"How do you think it will be after 2000?"

"I'll be out by then. I'm retiring in a few years, and probably will go back to the States."

He didn't seem to want to answer, but we had the distinct impression that things had gone down since the 1978 Treaty and that he feared the worst once the Panamanians took complete control.

We asked the same question of the French-Panamanian who had told us about the malaria. He laughed, shook his head, looked to the skies and said:

"I don't know, I just don't know," but again we had a feeling that he was doubtful of its future.

And what did the West Indian Panamanians themselves think?

"I'm retiring in three years aged 50," one told us, "I will have a good pension, I don't care what happens. Time will tell." Indeed it will.

Chapter 35

"I CAME OUT for the invasion and I kind of liked it so I stayed. I was in the Rangers, that's the elite Parachute Corps of the American Army. It's called the elite but we had guys who'd only been in it three weeks. They didn't know what they were doing. We had Americans shooting Americans. We had guys jumping into a doorway and jumping into each other."

"How many Americans died?"

"They say it was 20, but it was more than that. You know how you never hear the truth in these things. One of my friends died in my arms."

"When did you first know that the invasion would take place?"

"In September, after Noriega's men shot the rebels. We weren't allowed any communication even with our families. The telephones were out. They play with your mind. It's bad. They drown you and bring you back to life again, that kind of thing."

"Where did the invasion take place?"

"All around here. We hit all the Panamanian Defence Force bases round Panama, that's about 25 bases. We wanted to take the Commendavicia, but Noriega must have been informed because he got out."

"And now, looking back, how do you feel about it?"

"I don't know if it was worth those American lives. American Intelligence said that Noriega was giving orders to the P.D.F. to shoot Americans on sight and to go into Americans' homes on Christmas Day and shoot them, so something had to be done."

And what is it that you like about Panama City now?"

"It's relaxed for me now. I've got my girlfriend and we're planning on getting married. It's nice here and it's so cheap. If you get married here, you can get Panamanian citizenship."

And then his bus arrived, and this young, slim, crew-cut American shook hands, said it was nice meeting us, and went off with his Panamanian girlfriend.

He was the only person we met in Panama who had cast any doubt upon the wisdom of President Bush's decision to invade. Three months before the invasion, rebel officers had turned on Noriega; he phoned his own men, and they burst into his room and shot the rebels dead. General opinion seemed to be that it was a great pity that the rebels had not shot Noriega dead there and then.

"Great," was how another American described the invasion. "I've never seen so many American flags being flown."
"What, by the Americans here?"
"No, by the Panamanians. By the Panamanian people."

American interference in Central America is the subject of much criticism. I am not sufficiently expert on the subject of Central America, nor on International law, to comment in detail and I do accept that it must be very difficult to justify invading another country with a view to capturing its leader. It sets a dangerous precedent and leaves a sour taste in the mouth.

It must be remembered however that without the Americans, the canal may never have been built and Panama's importance on a world scale and the employment and well being of its people would have never reached the levels they have.

More importantly, it must be remembered that Panama had of its own free will transferred the legal rights and responsibility for the canal to the Americans, and, until the next century, the American are not just lawfully there, but are required to be there.

In these circumstances, when the leader of that country has seized power by removing the previous military leader, and has then annulled subsequent elections (held in May 1989) and is planning to kill your own country's citizens who are lawfully in that country, it does seem to me that for a President aware of these facts to stand back and do nothing on the grounds of non-interference in another country, would, to put it mildly, be a mistake. Theorising is all very well, but the answer to political problems cannot be provided by feeding theories into a computer and asking it to tell you what to do.

Imagine the furore if nothing had been done, a mass killing of Americans by Noriega's forces had taken place, and it was subsequently revealed that United States Intelligence had warned the President about it. It is easy to criticise and it is easy to theorise; the taking of decisions is a little harder.

The journey from Panama City to the border with Costa Rica was fairly dull. It was, in the main, flat, green/brown and bone dry, becoming more hilly and even a little jungly later on. After a day travelling west on a bus which resembled an American Greyhound, we reached the border. We were beginning to feel as if we were now at the stage of crossing countries off – this would be the fourth in under a week, but the first on the whole trip not to have an army.

Chapter 36

CO STA RICA is a popular holiday destination for Americans. This is no doubt because, as Central America goes, it is safe, democratic and civilised, because its population is predominantly white, and because it has both Pacific and Carribean beaches, reputedly wonderful National Parks and attractive scenery.

It's capital, San Jose, could be almost home from home for some American city folk. The streets are generally straight, Avenidas running east to west and Calles running north to south. As in New York, this is supposed to mean that you should avoid getting lost, although we did not find that it always worked.

Although blessed with some lovely old buildings – the Georgian-style National Theatre being one that particularly caught our eye – it seemed on the whole to be a modern, developed city, even if the number of high-rise buildings was down on what you would expect of an American city.

There were cinemas showing American films – we were lucky enough to see *Driving Miss Daisy* – and the city offered a range of restaurants more associated with the western world than Central America, including an excellent vegetarian restaurant.

We did not find it an inspiring city, and were pining for the beach, having not been to one since Montevideo, some three months before.

The train journey to the Caribbean coast is, according to the *South American Handbook*, "one of the most beautiful railway journeys anywhere". It must also be one of the slowest: the 100 mile journey from San Jose to Limon took around eight hours. It's beauty was what I would call natural and raw rather than classic.

We passed alongside jungle, coffee plantations, wooden huts with corrugated iron roofs and palm trees. It was always lush but

143

could be flat one minute and a steep drop literally from the trackside the next. I am afraid that the dramatic landscape which we had hoped for, did not materialise, the Colombian scenery no doubt having spoiled us. It is perhaps an unavoidable consequence of travel that the more you do, the more discerning you become and the less likely you are to be swept off your feet.

We spent a couple of days at Cahuita on the Carribean Coast. I have to say that it was disappointing. It was not helped by the frequent rain, and it was little consolation to be told that this was unusual before June when the rainy season properly got under way.

It may be that the weather overly affected our judgement, but the long, thin beaches, whose palm trees had fallen and were literally hanging over the water, were not our idea of paradise.

Nor were the restaurants. I have heard it said that the best waiters are those you have not, or have hardly, been aware of. That can only be true if, whilst having the meal, you were not aware of the fact that you were not aware of them. In Cahuita, we were painfully aware of the fact that we were hardly ever aware of them. They seemed to take being conspicuous beyond the level of acceptability. They were West Indians, as were many Cahuitans, and seemed to have the same sense of urgency and enthusiasm for work that we had witnessed in the Panamanian West Indians.

We were also a little put off by the number of drunk West Indians. Bars seemed to be open most of the day and it appeared that some of them hardly ever left. At all times of the day we would see people staggering around barely able to stand up.

Having said all of that, it had been a relaxing few days of swimming and reading, and we returned to San Jose feeling suitably rejuvenated.

Whilst Costa Rica had not exactly excited us, it had certainly been a pleasant, easy and safe country through which to travel. We were not expecting that the same could be said of the next one.

Chapter 37

AT THE COSTA RICAN–NICARAGUAN BORDER, we met an American Missionary. He worked in Costa Rica, Nicaragua and Panama, and liked Costa Rica the most.

"The people are very friendly and it's a lovely country, but there are problems. There's all this talk about democracy but there's a lot of corruption. The Election, I'm sorry to say, just changed one set of crooks for another."

"What about Panama?"

People always seemed to smile at the mention of Panama, and he was no exception.

"The Panamanians are very lazy. I have friends there and they admit they don't do the work they should do."

We were most anxious to know what he had to say about Nicaragua.

"Nicaragua is very poor. It is perhaps the poorest country in the Northern Hemisphere, worse even than Haiti."

The procedure at Nicaraguan customs was painfully slow. Everyone had to fill out a Currency Declaration Form which was then carefully scrutinised, and then everyone had to have all their luggage thoroughly searched. It seemed that the second task could not be commenced until everyone had gone through the first. The first posed a problem for us. It was Nicaraguan Law that every visitor had to change 60 US dollars into cordobas at the official exchange rate at the point of entry. We were planning to be in and out in a matter of days, and could ill afford to change so much.

The only alternative was to obtain a transit visa, which required us to change only 25 US dollars, but the catch was that it also required us to be out within 24 hours. We suspected that we could

145

not be, but decided to chance it. We would have a race on our hands.

"Getting through the border can take three to four hours," the Missionary explained, "but it's far more relaxed now than before the Election. Then the armed militia was here and people were roped in. The problem is that a lot of people bring bags of clothes from Costa Rica and try to avoid Nicaraguan duty, so they have to check every item."

The Election had taken place only a few months earlier, in February 1990. The governing party was the Sandinistas. The Sandinistas had obtained power not through the ballot box but by force, their revolution of 1978-9 eventually leading the ruling General Somoza to resign.

The Sandinista had subsequently called an Election, held in November 1984, won it with a small overall majority and appointed Daniel Ortego as President. The Americans considered the Poll to have been a sham, because a right-wing group, angry at the Sandinistas' refusal to meet its demands, had boycotted the Election.

The Sandinistas Government was plagued throughout its period of office by opposition from anti-Sandinista guerillas, the "contras", who had considerable American support. Despite the strain on its resources, it seems to be an accepted fact that the Sandinista Government had made significant improvements particularly in the country's health and education, and the Sandinistas went into the Election as favourites.

The Polls were even more up the spout than those for the British Election of April 1992, which, as I write, have just been held. The winner by a very clear majority was the opposition party led by Violetta Barrios de Chamorro.

"The Polls had said that the Sandinistas would win," explained the Missionary, "but interestingly one market research company did predict the winner. And do you know how they did it?"
We indicated that we did not.
"Well, they checked on which newspaper the people read, and if it was *La Prensa*, the opposition newspaper, they put that person down for Violetta even if they said Ortego. They thought, obviously correctly, that people were too frightened to say that they would vote against the Government."

146

Shaun amongst the locals in Quito.

Baby carriers in Quito, Ecuador.

Our guide and some locals in the Jungle near Mishuali, Ecuador.

Breathtakingly dramatic Colombian scenery.

Centre of Managua, Nicaragua.

Ladies in typical Guatamalan dress – Chichistenango.

Jo preparing the sign for the hitch-hike to San Francisco.

Shaun reunited with his friend Bob Lightowlers in Eugene, Oregon.

"In fact," he continued, "it was a landslide victory. Probably even more so than disclosed. On the TV they started giving the result as percentages rather than numbers, so that it sounded better for the Government. After it became clear that the Sandinistas had been roundly defeated, the TV simply stopped giving results. And now the new President has got a problem: she's keeping Daniel Ortego's brother as Head of the Army so that he can supervise the Contra's disarming, but the Contras and the US are up in arms with her about it. So there's still problems."

After several hours, we finally departed for Managua. The journey started round the vast Lake Nicaragua and continued alongside very dry, barren landscape in which stood thin and haggard horses and cows. The few properties we saw were wooden and were really no more than shacks.

And then the bus broke down. The driver and a few passengers fiddled with the engine, and after little under an hour we were on the move again. It was dark by the time we reached Managua. The door to the luggage compartment then got stuck so we all waited around until the driver eventually worked out another way of retrieving our belongings.

And then the gates through which we would leave what was laughingly called a "bus station" were locked and we waited another 15 minutes before somebody produced the key. It was very clear that Nicaraguans operated at two speeds, the faster of which was very slow.

It was unnerving walking round Managua. It seemed inconceivable that it was a capital city: almost devoid of traffic and people, it had the feel of a ghost town.

Our task of finding somewhere to stay was not helped by the fact that there seemed to be no street names. Finally, we found a "Hospedaje" (accommodation within a family home). We had not seen a single shop on the way and were starving.

"Where can we buy some food?" we asked the lady at the Hospedaje.

"Next door," she replied.

This confused us – next door looked like a house, and we heard the TV on and could see people inside watching it – but we were sure that we had understood her correctly.

147

We knocked on the door. A young girl answered. Sure enough, there in the sitting room, was a small counter and fridge. So that is why we had seen no shops – they are in people's homes. We purchased some bread and milk to tide us over, and soon came to realise that this was the first country we had been to where the obtaining of food is a challenge in itself, such is the shortage of it. Many foods are apparently the subject of rationing.

We took a stroll, walking down the middle of the streets in which children were playing. The houses were constructed out of wood, tin and corrugated iron, and many had gaps so that you could see inside them. We found what would presumably be classed as a restaurant and endured tasteless chicken soup with an egg in it, and oily chicken, chips and rice, washed down with beer, there being no juices, shakes or mineral water and normal water not being safe. The "restaurant's" toilet was a hole in the ground.

It was not only food that was rationed; so too was the water. We were fortunate to arrive on a day in which our Hospedaje had some; two days a week it did not.

Because of the 24 hour deadline, we would have to wake early in the morning, but I wanted to sample Managua's night life, or rather find out if it had any. Only a 10 minute walk from the slum area in which we were staying, I came across a large pyramid-shaped hotel complete with swimming pool and several restaurants. People were tucking into a delicious looking buffet of chicken, fish, meat and salad. It was like suddenly entering another world. Other than that, however, the night life of this capital city – I kept having to tell myself that it was one – appeared to be non existent.

It was already warm when we woke at 6.00 the next morning and the girls in our house were getting ready for school. We walked towards the centre and intended catching a bus to the Cathedral. At least we did until we saw one. It was so crowded that people were literally hanging out of it. Given that we had all our luggage on us, the decision to take a taxi instead was not one that took us very long to make.

Managua has had, to put it mildly, a most unfortunate 20th century. Firstly, it was destroyed by an earthquake in 1931. Five years later, it suffered a serious fire. Then, having been rebuilt, the centre was destroyed by another earthquake in December 1972 which left 40,000 people dead. Finally the Sandinistra Revolution

148

of 1978-9 all but finished the city off. As a result, you see very few buildings, and a tall Bank of America building, which was probably one of many prior to 1972, stood out like a sore thumb.

The Cathedral was in ruins: devoid of roof or pews, grass and weeds grew inside it around the marble pillars, its stone walls were full of huge cracks and the clock showed the time as 1.29 as it had done for some 18 years, recalling the exact time of the Cathedral's destruction.

As we wandered round, a few young boys, aged perhaps five or six, came up to us begging. They were filthy, their shirts and trousers were torn and their feet were bare. When we told them that we were from England, one made a notion of firing a gun. Had he seen the Poll Tax riots on TV, we wondered.

Near the Cathedral, horribly thin cows and horses scratched around in a miserable, seemingly hopeless search for grass. The roads were more like paths and were full of cracks and devoid of motor vehicles. The housing, as in the area of our Hospedaje, was no more than shacks or huts of wood, tin and corrugated iron thrown together in an apparently random fashion.

It was without doubt the poorest, most deserted, most depressing and most unfortunate capital city either of us had ever seen. It seemed to be a city without hope. Or at least it seemed without hope, for it could not really be said that it seemed to be a city at all.

Chapter 38

IT WAS ONLY AROUND a 150 mile journey to the Honduras border. We had to be there by 2.00 pm and felt that our arrival at the Managua bus station at 9.00 am would ensure that we would be.

It had been impossible to find out the bus times in advance and, even at the station, information was hard to come by. People often did not listen when we talked to them; they seemed down-hearted and it was easy to understand why.

At the same time, some did try to be helpful and sometimes were, but it was not done in the warm, smiling, cheery manner of the Peruvians, the Panamanians and the Costa Ricans. There were a few beggars, although they looked embarrassed to be doing it. We suspected that many more really needed to, but their pride would not allow it.

The 100 mile journey to Estelli took three hours and cost 30 pence. The next bus from there to Ocotal, the border town, was not until 2.00 pm, the time our passports were stamped. It looked as if we may have blown it. There was no alternative: we would have to hitch hike.

"You must take a taxi to the Pan-American Highway," we were told, "it's a good hitching position."

We had been told about "good hitching positions" before, and feared the worst. This time it was good. The problem was that it was too good; four other groups of hitch hikers were already there, including a hitch hiking combination I had never seen anywhere before, a mother and baby.

"How long till the border?" we asked, barely disguising our desperation.

"About an hour," replied one.

"A good two hours," replied another.

We flagged down a taxi driver and offered him $15 to take us to the border. He told us it was a two hour trip and he'd take us for $20. If it's a two hour trip, we thought, we'll miss the 24 hours deadline anyway. He had inadvertently blown his chances. Talking of chances, ours now looked almost non-existent.

Just after the taxi left, and as were beginning to curse our tightness, a van pulled up. Two girls got in the front, a chap and the lady with the baby in the back. The driver nodded at us. Without further thought, we took this as our invitation and clambered aboard.

And off into the unknown we went. Our driver must have picked 12 more people up in the next hour, some only going very short distances. We wondered if it was common practice in Nicaragua for those few fortunate enough to afford transport to help out the majority who cannot.

"It's half an hour to Ocotal, then 15 minutes more to the border," he explained when he finally dropped us.

It was 2.30 pm. The deadline had passed. We now had a more serious problem: were we going to reach the border before it closed? Nobody knew what time this was, but some suggested it could be around 4.00 pm.

The landscape was harsh and dry. Far more importantly, traffic was scarce. Then a pick up arrived. It had benches on either side which each sat six, and standing room in the middle. Another fine example of Nicaraguan public transport.

"There's a bus to the border at 3.30 pm," various people including the driver informed us at Ocotal bus station, "and the border closes at 5.00 pm."

Perfect, we thought, perfect. And sure enough, at 3.30 pm, not one, but two, buses arrived.

"Is this the one to the border?" we asked an official.
"No."
"Oh, so it's the other one."
"No."
"Which is the bus to border?"
"There isn't one."
"But there's one at 3.30 pm."
"No, the next one is in the morning – 6.00 am."

We could not believe it.

"But the border is open till 5.00 pm," we exclaimed.

The official confirmed that this was true.

"So why no bus?"

It was no use. No amount of exclaiming can suddenly make public servants logical, and it was certainly not going to at Ocotal bus station.

It would have to be a taxi. We stomped angrily and aggressively around Ocotal; not a taxi in sight. We picked on a chap at random.

"Are there any taxis to the border?"

"Ah, no," he paused . . . "but I can get my friend – he's a taxi driver. He'll get you there in 15 minutes. Wait at the corner."

Ten minutes later, a van pulled up. The chap said this was what he meant by the taxi. We were beginning to wonder about him.

"We can take you for $20."

"$20! Far too much."

"But it's far – 30 minutes."

"But you said 15."

"No – more."

"Then we'll be too late anyway."

"No, it takes 15 minutes."

This was turning into a pantomime.

"You just said 30."

"No, my friend will drive very fast."

By the end of the conversation we had stopped wondering about him. There seemed no doubt about it: he was an out and out crook. We gave up. We would stay in Ocotal and take the consequences tomorrow.

There was a hotel for $2, which seemed very reasonable until we saw what you got for it: a bare room, just bigger than the bed, no sheets and a dusty and dirty mattress.

"Can we see the showers?"

"No."

"Why's that?"

"We don't have any."

We left. The next place was equally cramped but had a shower; we were past caring about anything else and took it.

What a day it had been. Interesting, without a doubt, but ultimately very frustrating. Despite striving desperately to meet the deadline, and coming so close, we would actually end up arriving around 18 hours late. For some reason, although it probably should have done, it didn't bother us in the slightest.

The journey to the border the next morning was through the hilliest and most attractive scenery we had experienced in Nicaragua, and, contrary to what everybody had told us, took 45 minutes. The moment of truth had arrived: will our exit be refused? Will we have to pay $60, or (God forbid) will we have to call the British Embassy to bail us out?

We joined a short queue. Our passports were stamped. We tried to appear nonchalant, but expected to be called back when it dawned on them we had overstayed. And then customs expressed no interest in our bags and waved us on.

"Is that it?" we thought. It was, incredibly and in minutes, without even so much as a raised eyebrow, we were no longer in Nicaragua. The poverty and deprivation, the chaos, the barren landscape, the deserted streets of the capital and the begging children were a thing of the past. Unless Honduras had them too.

Chapter 39

WE NOTICED A DIFFERENCE immediately on crossing the border. The Hondurans in the one bar at the border were cheerful, smiling and relaxed, sporting Honduran hats and looking altogether cleaner, healthier and better dressed than their Nicaraguan counterparts.

Changing money provided two surprises. Firstly, instead of being set upon by a mass of greasy spivs with wads of notes and pocket calculators, there were only a few money changers, and they could not have been more polite.

Secondly, the exchange rate was $1 to four Honduran Limpiras. It seemed strange to have notes which were actually worth something and to have so few of them. We had become accustomed to carrying around bundles of notes which might together be worth around 10 pence. So valuable were the notes that Honduras even had coins. We could not recall the last time we had had them.

The marked contrast continued for the four hour journey to the capital, Tegucigalpa. Where Nicaragua had been harsh, dry and generally flat, this journey took us through lush, hilly terrain dominated by pine trees, which, it came as no surprise to discover, is the Honduran National Tree. It was certainly not land that would be suitable for agriculture; indeed, less than one quarter of Honduras' land is cultivated, nearly half of it being forest.

Tegucigalpa had an Arab feel: dreadful roads full of bumps and potholes, hooting horns, an enormous market and a generally bustling atmosphere. Even outside the market itself, there were still endless market stalls along the pavement.

It did not however feel claustrophobic, largely I think on account of having been built at and around the foot of the El Picacho

Mountain. It was certainly not a touristy city; indeed it was extremely difficult even to find a post card.

There was nothing to delay our much needed progress and we took a bus north to Honduras' second largest city, San Pedro Sula. I was engrossed in Jeffrey Archer's *A Matter of Honour*, but whenever I looked, the journey was through forest, and I suspect it almost always was.

A solicitor whom I had spoken to in Bath who had also toured South and Central America after completing his Articles, albeit some 10 years previously, had included amongst his few strongest recommendations, the Ruins of Copan.

The Ruins of Copan lie in North-Western Honduras close to the border with Guatemala. Their location is no coincidence; Copan was one of the cities of the Mayan civilisation which evolved in around AD 100 mainly in Guatemala although also in El Salvador and Honduras.

Amongst many other achievements, the Mayans developed a calendar (a month comprising 20 days), grew lavish crops, built numerous temples and statues and developed many independent City States.

Archaeologists are still digging and researching at Copan, but the ruins of some 15 temples have already been discovered below ground level. The statues were of their Mayan rulers – priests and nobles – and the position of their feet, we were told, showed whether or not they had ever killed anybody.

It seemed that there was a certain disregard for life amongst the Mayans and possibly even an element of glorying in death. Nothing illustrated this more than a rather peculiar sport: players had to prevent a heavy ball hitting the ground, and could only do so by use of their elbows. This absurd sounding activity was enjoyed by thousands of spectators who would then vote on who the best player was.

If the game itself seems to leave something to be desired, the prize for the "Best Player" was surely counter-productive: he was decapitated. Apparently, however, the prospect of such a reward acted as a positive spur to greater elbowing, and was accepted with pleasure and pride. The Mayan male ego clearly knew no bounds. It was therefore not without relief that I learned that, after a Golden

Age of several centuries, the Mayan civilisation had faded into insignificance in around AD 1000.

We travelled to Guatemala City in a bus driven by a Guatemalan in which he was transporting prospective American tour guides whom we had met at the ruins. Both he and the Americans were wildly enthusiastic about Guatemala but our first experience of it was a bad one.

It could not have occurred any earlier; the border official queried our visa.

"These are not valid," he told us matter-of-factly, "they are too old, they are only valid for 30 days from issue."

"No, its for 30 days from entry," we replied, "that was what the Guatemalan Embassy in London told us."

"These are not valid. You must pay $5 for each visa."

$10 may not seem much, but this was intensely irritating. We were almost certain the customs official would pocket it – and $10 is probably a few days wages for the average Guatemalan – and with our rapidly dwindling resources it was not insignificant for us either.

When we asked for written confirmation that the visa was invalid, he refused to give it and when we asked why, he refused to give a reason.

And what did the Guatemalan driver and the Americans who had so extolled Guatemala's virtues have to say about this? It was the only time on the trip that they fell silent. We were not impressed.

Chapter 40

OUR SECOND INCIDENT in Guatemala was even worse. It occurred the next day in Guatemala City.

We went out to obtain some Quetzales. A young Guatemalan approached us in the street and started chatting. He seemed friendly enough, and having had it pummelled into us the day before how wonderful the Guatemalans were (save during and immediately after the border incident), we chatted back. He spoke good English, having apparently lived in the States.

He told us that a friend of his could give us a better rate than the Banks. We walked a long way to an office, but the friend wasn't there. Then he remembered another friend who could also beat the Bank. We walked to another building.

"I will have to go up. You can't be seen there because we are not supposed to change money with foreigners."

"No problem," we thought. But there was a problem. The friend had to see our money before parting with his. Embarrassing though it is to write it, I handed over $90 cash to this man whom we had simply met in the street under an hour ago.

Jo had smelt a rat even before, but for some reason I had not. I told her confidently that he could be trusted, but it was with considerable relief that I saw him emerging from the door he had gone through a few minutes earlier. My faith in human nature was restored and I gave Jo a look which said, "How could you doubt my judgment?". She gave me one back which said "Very easily and I still do."

She was right. Our "friendly" Guatemalan produced a cheque. "My friend didn't have the cash on him. We just take this cheque to a Bank and get the cash for you."

I was back to doubting again. We headed off to the Bank.

"I just have to see a friend," he told us after a few minutes. "Can we go to the Bank first?"

"No, I have to catch her quickly."

We entered a building and approached the lifts.

"You wait here, I won't be a minute."

"It's O.K., I'll come with you."

"No, you stay here."

For the first time, he was showing signs of anger. The stench of rat was now overpowering.

I went up in the lift with him; we got out and he went through a glass door and came immediately back again.
"She's not there."

Well, there's a surprise. We went down, met up with Jo and carried on walking. This man is not getting more than a foot away from me, I thought. Jo and I kept looking at each other. We both knew that we were dealing with a crook.

"Where's the Bank?" we asked persistently.

"Just a bit further," he kept replying.

And then I grabbed him and threatened him. He looked a bit frightened, which came, I must confess, as rather a pleasant surprise.

Jo kept giving me signals but I wasn't sure what they meant. Then she dropped back. I now had to keep my eyes on both of them. For a few seconds, Jo disappeared. Then I spotted her, pleading desperately with a local.

We walked to a market where no doubt he hoped to lose me in the crowd, and passed slow-moving buses where the split second he tried to leap on I was ready to as well. Serious though it was, I was beginning to feel as if I was in a movie: "Englishman Tracks Guatemalan in Tale of International Espionage".

Finally, I saw Jo with a man in uniform. Presuming, correctly as it transpired, that he was a policeman, I grabbed the thief by the scruff of the neck and frog-marched him towards the arms of the law. Just as I did so, he said: "I am sorry. My mother is sick," and he handed me the $90. I had not even realised that he still had it.

In the relief of seeing the money again, I relaxed my grip and he got away.

A crowd had gathered round. The policeman looked gormless; everyone else looked interested. Nobody looked concerned. Poor Jo had been tearing her hair out shouting at people to help us and receiving no response.

So much for the wonderful Guatemalans. We had now met three: one of them had almost certainly stolen from us, another had nearly deprived us of almost a week's spending money and the other had charged us a lot more than the usual fare for a trip he was doing anyway, spent the entire journey telling us what a wonderful country Guatemala is, but was happy to stand by and do nothing as we were made to pay twice for entering it. Then, to cap it all, not a single person seemed remotely concerned at the fact that a Guatemalan had stolen from foreign visitors. That is not my idea of wonderful.

With experiences like those, it would be hard for us to have liked Guatemala City. I suspect however that it would have been hard anyway. It struck us both as flat, modern, Americanised and characterless. Traffic was heavy and smog a problem.

In four days there, we met a chap who told us he had been robbed of his rucksack at knife point, and, admittedly rather foolishly, everything including passport and travellers cheques had been in it, and a girl who had had her rucksack stolen from underneath her feet when on a bus.

To say that we were happy to leave would be an understatement.

Chapter 41

"I'VE LOVED EVERY MINUTE of it, the people are wonderful, so friendly; the walking is so beautiful and the markets and the costumes fantastic."

So said an English girl we'd met who'd spent a month learning Spanish in Antigua and then some time living in the villages of Northern Guatemala.

No country can be judged by its capital city nor its people by its capital's inhabitants. It is harder for city folk to be friendly; time is generally of the essence, it is often noisy, crowded and polluted and the whole atmosphere is hardly conducive to feeling warm towards your fellow citizens.

It was therefore with the promise of seeing a wholly different sort of Guatemalan, as well as some beautiful scenery, that we left Guatemala City for the village of Chichistenango in Guatemala's Northern Highlands.

The four hour journey transported us through lush, green countryside past buildings constructed out of the leaves of palm trees with thatched roofs. Many Indians were either walking or sitting along the roadside, sporting costumes which were a kaleidoscope of colours – purple, red, yellow, green and pink – generally striped and which included wide, brightly coloured belts and headgear.

We could not recall ever seeing so much sign of life on a roadside. Often there was not a building in sight, and it was hard to see where they had all emerged from, or where they would end up.

Guatemala has a higher proportion of pure Indians – over 50% – than any other Central American country. Elsewhere, they were either killed off by disease or inter-married with the Spanish. It is only in Guatemala that their languages and culture could be said to truly live on.

Some of the land was flat and cultivated, and we sometimes saw neat rows of maize, cotton or vegetables. The final part of the trip, approaching Chichi (as it is conveniently called) was by far the most exciting: the climbs were steep, the bends sharp, the view of narrow valleys spectacular and the old and packed bus was struggling.

Chichi seemed a million miles from Guatemala City: built around an enormous square plaza, which you enter through an old low, painted arch from what could euphemistically be called its "main road", its buildings were low and mainly white, and in short it was the haven of peace and tranquility for which we yearned.

It was a different story the next day: thousands of Indians flocked into the town from the surrounding hills for the Thursday Market. The whole plaza was awash with colour: not simply of the Indians' own apparel but seemingly virtually everything that was for sale as well, from belts to hammocks and table cloths to purses.

It was a much more enjoyable market than that of Otovalo, almost certainly because, being more remote, it was far less touristy. And, yes, the Guatemalans were indeed much friendlier here than in Guatemala City, and than the Ecuadorian Indians of Otovalo. Bargaining was keen but not intense, and the less pushy manner of these locals certainly paid off for them, as we, and I have no doubt many others, came away with a stack of souvenirs and presents.

It was in another almost unpronounceable town that we spent the night; Quezaltenango. The Guatemalans had a short name for this one too: Xela (pronounced Shayla). You had to find out the shortened versions or you would never get on the right bus; the locals did not appear to refer to towns by their full name, nor could they understand foreigners' attempts to pronounce them.

Xela is Western Guatemala's foremost city with a population of around 120,000, and apparently it has a wonderful plaza in the centre. We arrived late and were off again at 5.00 am, and sadly had no chance to explore.

It was our last day in Guatemala. The journey to the Mexican border, we were led to believe, should take around five hours. This was surprising as it only looked on the map to be a distance of around 100 miles. However, having had the bus to ourselves at Zela, it then stopped so frequently on the roadside to pick up Indians that we soon wondered if five hours was perhaps on the quick side.

The journey to Huehetenango took us through the most orderly cultivated fields we had seen anywhere on the trip. After Huehetenango, however, the contrast could hardly have been more drastic. The hills were a much darker green and rose steeply from the roadside, the bends were sharp and, after climbing quickly, we could see from the bus the dramatic drops into the valley.

We finally reached the border town of La Mesilla after some six hours on the bus. It was then a stretch of "no mans land" of over two miles to the Mexican border post for which, in no mood to hang about any longer, we took a taxi.

Having already obtained the Mexican Visa in Guatemala City (they are not provided at the border) we were through the border control and then customs, in a matter of minutes. After an uncertain start, to say the least, Guatemala and its people had grown on us. We both suspected, however, that it represented for us a classic example of the contrast between city and country in which our personal preference for countryside determined both our mood and our impression .

Chapter 42

CENTRAL AMERICA comprises seven countries: the five we had just been through plus El Salvador and Belize.

Mexico is several times larger than all of them put together, although putting it into context, it is only around one quarter of the area of the United States.

There are four main road routes to the US border, all of which involve going via Mexico City. We would be using the Pacific Coastline route, so as to arrive into West California.

The only drawback was that this was the longest route: around 2,000 miles. We now had only three weeks left, and really wanted to be reaching the US border within a week.

There was a very large, clean bus station at the border and, something we had not seen for a long time, a timetable showing not only destinations but prices as well. More "United States" American than Central American, we thought.

The "bus" itself, however, heralded an immediate return to the ways of Central America: it was simply a van with a bench on either side for about 12 people, and everybody else stood and had luggage squeezed in between them.

It took three buses and around 16 hours to reach Oaxaca. Sleep was more off than on, and not helped by frequent stops for armed soldiers to check on people's passports.

We contemplated trying to go straight on to Mexico City but, wandering into Oaxaca's centre to change some money, I was rather struck by the town, and so we decided to stay, make up for lost sleep and catch the 7.00 am bus the next day.

The main plaza of Oaxaca was as fine a plaza as you will see. We were struck both by its enormity and by its beauty: lovely arched buildings, trees dominated and there were French style cafes with tables and chairs outside. Perhaps even more important than what there was was what there was not: the whole area was traffic free.

We were just settling down to enjoy a bite to eat and watch the orchestra which was on the verge of performing in the centre when, without warning, the heavens opened. We sought refuge in the 17th-century Cathedral, also in the plaza. This, it must be said, was disappointing. It had extremely ugly and extremely lengthy strip lights on the pillars, the ceiling was yellow with age and in general it had clearly seen better days. A lot of people were crying.

When the downpour ceased, which was fairly quickly, we went a few blocks from the plaza to visit the Church of Santa Domingo which was strongly recommended in the *South American Handbook*.

I have no hesitation in saying that the Church at Santa Domingo in Oaxaca is quite astonishing. It was like entering another world. The altar was literally covered in gold-leaf its entire width and to a height of what must have been around 20 metres.

Down the side of the Church were six high arches, all of the same size, inside each of which stood, sat or lay life-size statues of Christ in various positions, the common denomination of which was that they all looked painful. Each statue was enclosed within a huge glass container so that direct physical contact was out of the question. In parts, the ceiling was covered in gold, but in the main it was relatively plain – white with regular dark spots – and did not distract from the majestic appeal of the altar.

All around the Church were figures in gold, apparently depicting the descendants of the family of Santa Domingo de Guzman as well of course as the usual Biblical scenes. It was the altar, however, which had left us gasping. We sat near to the front of the Church and just stared at it almost in disbelief. A priest started talking from behind a table in front of the altar. Unfortunately there was an echo and he was talking quickly and, hard though we tried, we could not understand any of it.

A group of surprisingly scruffily dressed men were preparing to play their violins. What a pleasant civilised occasion, we thought, and how fortunate we had not had the money for the Mexico City bus.

164

And then the violinists started. We recognised the tune immediately: *Here comes the bride.*

What a strange tune to play, we thought. Or at least we did until I glanced behind.

"Oh my God," I said to Jo, the shock producing an unfortunate turn of phrase.

"What?"

"Look behind you."

We looked at each other and both sniggered slightly.

"What shall we do?" Jo whispered.

"I think we should stay."

"How embarrassing."

"Yes, but interesting."

The bride was moving slowly up the aisle, dressed in a traditional white wedding dress and veil. Her escort was a young man (clearly not her father) who looked a bit of a wide-boy and was wearing a fawn jacket, blue shirt and a flowery tie. The numbers had increased hugely since we had arrived. Some men wore ties, but many didn't; some were in leather jackets. The ladies wore summery shirts or dresses, but there was not a hat in sight.

When the bride had completed her walk, both she and the groom sat down on chairs at the table behind which the priest was standing. The groom, sporting white shirt, bow tie and dinner jacket, looked to be a marked improvement on the "Beatles man" whom we assumed must be the best man.

The priest spoke some more incomprehensible words, and then the congregation stood up. This presented another dilemma. Whilst the general apparel was not of the standard expected of an English wedding, it would be fair to assume that, in vests, shorts and training shoes, we cannot have failed to arouse attention, and perhaps even suspicion.

Applying the "When in Rome" principle, I thought that we too should stand, but Jo did not, considering that the full extent of our state of undress might not be clear if we remained seated. We remained seated.

Then in true wedding tradition, a baby started crying and, shortly afterwards, a boy of perhaps three years set of on a frolic of his own heading towards the altar. Mutterings of disapproval could be heard, before a girl, who did not seem much older, was dispatched to retrieve him. Another little boy tried the same trick but by now parents were alert to the possibility and his mother's outstretched arm just managed to yank him back.

Our attention reverted to the main event in time to see a long white necklace being placed over the bride's head. The violinists played briefly, the priest spoke again and then the bride and groom, staring into the space in front of them, rather than at each other, divested themselves of their independence and sounded pretty scared to be doing so.

On completion of the formalities, the man to our right turned and shook our hands, and then the lady on the left did the same and also gave Jo a bowl of rice with a veil.

Bride, groom, wide-boy and other members of the "wedding party elite" went outside for the inevitable photo session and we took the first opportunity to depart.

Chapter 43

WE SPENT THE WHOLE of the next day on a bus.

Unfortunately it was not an attractive journey. The landscape was harsh and uncultivated, and sightings of animals, trees and buildings were extremely rare. The most memorable part of the journey for us was a stretch of land on which grew enormous cactus plants; there were literally thousands of them, grown to a height of perhaps 20 feet.

Mexico City is the most populated city in the world. Its 20 million inhabitants comprise one quarter of the country's population. Beyond this fact, and that it had appalling traffic and smog problems, we knew nothing about it.

Even the bus terminal seemed to be bigger than some towns: it took us 20 minutes to walk to the taxi stands. There was a long queue. After about 30 minutes we reached the front of it and acquired our taxi tickets from a kiosk. But this was not the end of it; we then had to join another queue to actually get a taxi itself. This took another 30 minutes. Welcome back to the Big City . . . 1 hour 20 minutes and we hadn't even left the bus station.

When we finally did, what did we see? A lot of traffic, rubbish piled up on most street corners, dark sombre buildings, not as many high-rises as we had expected, and two men engaging openly in homosexual activity.

The first hotel we tried was cramped and seedy, the second a relative haven but too dear at £10 and the third adequate for half the price. We took a stroll but by 7.30 it was dark. I had an urge, a frequent occurrence, for a pint of milk, but could not find one anywhere, even in a supermarket.

We were becoming fairly fed up with Mexican food. If you don't like maize, then you are in trouble, and I don't like maize. Jo could eat it, albeit without much pleasure, but I was finding it positively unpleasant. It was not just the taste but also the texture that was off putting.

For tunately, however, the tostadas in the restaurant we selected that evening were good. Tostadas are toasted tortillas filled with chicken, beans and lettuce. Although tortillas are maize pancakes, the process of toasting them made the texture bearable and the taste seemed to be overshadowed by that of the filling.

We also had some tamales that evening but wished we hadn't. Tamales comprise a mincemeat and bean mixture wrapped in maize and banana leaves, and boiled. It was soggy and unappetising looking and one bite was all that we could manage.

Our most enjoyable Mexican food to date had been the tacos and enchilados. Whilst, inevitably, both comprise meat or chicken (and in the latter case chillies) wrapped in maize the process of frying it seemed to improve both taste and texture no end.

Costa Rico had provided our last coastal swim, and we were ready for another, there being little else that can rejuvenate weary minds and limbs so quickly. After another 16 hours bus journey, most of it through the night, speedy rejuvenation was just what was needed. Mazatlan provided it.

Despite being Mexico's largest port on the Pacific Ocean, and the commercial and industrial centre of the west, its setting was attractive, the air seemed fresh and its beaches, lined with palm trees, were peaceful. We spent the afternoon swimming, sunbathing and eating fish salad at an open air wooden thatched "restaurant" on the beach.

Our hotel was only two blocks from the beach; we enjoyed its large en suite room with two double beds, its very hot water, its garden with palm trees and its peace and quiet. We walked into the warm Mazatlan evening feeling clean, healthy and refreshed. A Tequila Sunrise or two followed by a good meal with a bottle of wine would be just the ticket.

Try though we did, it proved impossible to find a Tequila Sunrise, and not only in Mazatlan. Just as in Ecuador where we had failed to sample any banana wine – "its disgusting, much better to have Argentinian or Chilean" – the national drink was conspicuous by its absence.

However the meal more than compensated. It was by a long way our best meal in Mexico. If you find yourself in, or even near Mazatlan, go to Memucas (having first checked that it still has the same chef).

An enormous seafood grill was placed in the middle of our table. There were coals inside a fish-shaped hollow earthenware pot and on top was the most wonderful array of food; oysters with cheese, oysters with tomato, shrimps, king prawns, white fillet of fish, lobster, onions and peppers. With a support act of salad, delicious bread rolls and a bottle of Sana Tomas in an ice bucket, we felt we had been temporarily transported to Heaven.

It is a feature of travelling, or certainly of travelling without pre-arranged bookings and on limited funds, that it can plunge you to the depths of despair and then salvage you from them and provide occasions of supreme joy such as in the Mazatlan Restaurant.

It is this very uncertainty, this up and down characteristic, which can transform you from feeling ill, filthy, hungry, desperate and angry, to feeling rejuvenated and immensely contented in a matter of hours that explains in part the appeal of travelling. There is no doubt that this is part of its appeal, and no doubt also that this is why relatively few people do it. If you can have a daily shower, a roof over your head and three square meals a day, why on earth give them up? Is the answer perhaps that if you know what is going to happen, and every day is much the same, then what is the point of it all? Where will the kicks come from? Where is the sense of achievement? And how do you know you are content until you have tried some alternatives?

The meal in Mazatlan may not have seemed so heavenly had it not been preceded by a cramped night bus of broken sleep and inadequate food, and had we not known that another night bus was to follow.

The journey to the Mexican border town of Tijuana took 26 hours: from lunch time until the next afternoon. Some of the route was a sand desert with low lying shrubs about a foot apart, all of it was harsh, the few trees were devoid of leaves, people sat on stalls down the centre of the bus rendering the stretching of legs an impossibility, the air conditioning remained on through the night and a member of the Narcotics Squad insisted on looking inside my money belt, passport and left shoe.

169

It was with relief that we finally reached Tijuana but the relief was to be short-lived. Tijuana is probably the most visited city in the world. Not, as we were soon to discover, on account of its beauty or its people, but quite simply because it marks the Mexican-US border. Some 35 million people visit from the US every year. I do not know how many of them go elsewhere in Mexico as well, but the idea that people's opinions on Mexico could be formed simply on the basis of Tijuana is a frightening one indeed.

We needed two things: a place to cash travellers cheques and a hotel. Lots of "Casa de Cambios" advertised no commission, but only on entry did you discover that they only took cash. The first hotel we tried was run down, expensive and insisted on cash immediately.

We could not help but be struck by how morose and unfriendly all the people seemed to be. They were either obese or skinny and many looked as if they had indulged in illegal substances.

The hotels all had a dirty, sleazy look and many had what we assumed were prostitutes in swimsuits wandering in and out. Shocked and distraught at such a repulsive town, we even tried ringing Karen, a friend in San Diego, to see if we could go straight there. She wasn't in, so we resigned ourselves to a night in Tijuana, obtained cash and a bottle of Tequila at an off-licence and booked into a passable hotel whose owner produced the first smile we had seen in the town.

Everything was loud and glitzy. Flashing lights sought to entice you into the bars and nightclubs from which dreadful disco music boomed. Signs proclaimed "Come and join the fun at . . .". No thank you.

We finally found a bar where we could hear ourselves speak. It was a long dark room with velvet seats, and a TV showing five-a-side soccer. A few men drank at it in silence and apparent misery. We ordered a Tequila Sunrise – the first we had found – and a Margarita.

"Three dollars fifty," said the fat, unsmiling waiter as he plonked them in front of us. We gave him five dollars and he put one dollar fifty on the tray. I picked it up.

"Thanks very much," he said sarcastically and walked off throwing the bill at our table.

"The only tip I'd give you is to learn some manners," I said inwardly, and could see that Jo agreed with what I had not said.

There is little I find more nauseating than the thought of being seen purely in terms of money. Tijuana was consumerism gone crazy – the worst elements of the States, Hong Kong, and Manila rolled together – outwardly loud, glitzy, carefree and fun, but inwardly so shallow, miserable, sad and depressing.

"Come and join the money roller coaster," the adverts should have said with a Government Health Warning about the risk of damage to your soul.

Chapter 44

"YOUR ACTIONS AND CONVERSATION are being recorded on video tape," proclaimed one sign at US Customs.

"Wait your turn here," ordered another, and we dutifully did, being careful neither to do nor to say anything which might incriminate us.

Having waited our turn for some time, we came face to face with a big, fat, grey haired, balding, bearded American Customs Official who had more badges than "Stormin' Norman" and was not the sort of person you would want to be face to face with for any longer than strictly necessary.

"Where's your 994s?" he exclaimed after grabbing our passports.

"What the hell's a 994?" I thought but he was not a man to say a thing like that to, so we just gave blank looks.

"Hey, these guys haven't got a 994," he shouted to his mate, and we half expected people to move away as if we were some sort of outcasts or carried a dreadful disease.

"You gotta get in that line over there and get your 994."

We joined the other queue, but it wasn't moving and we were still none the wiser about the 994. We went back to the fat man. "Why do we need these 994s, we've got a visa?"

"Don't ask questions, just get in line."

In all of South and Central America, where freedoms are allegedly denied, customs officials apparently corrupt and violence and aggression supposedly commonplace, we had never encountered such heavy handed treatment, such interrogation and such stress. If this is democracy, I thought, give me anarchy any day.

We finally reached the front of the queue for the all powerful 994. Three American officials were chewing gum and being generally arrogant and uncouth.

"I ain't even got time to wipe my arse around here," said one, and the others agreed, which was fortunate given that they too were presumably on video.

"Got a ticket out?" one asked, engaging the American habit of asking questions in the shortest form possible.

"No, we're going to buy one in Seattle."

"Got funds?"

"Yes," we replied, thinking two can play at this game.

"How long here?"

"About three weeks."

"Got any evidence?"

We showed him letters from employers and filled out a form. They studied them. It reminded me of notes my mother used to give me to say I couldn't eat certain school food. I would wait tentatively while some enormous dinner-lady, usually called Ethel, determined whether I would suffer cold runny eggs with cold tinned tomatoes, and I remember how deeply your gratitude had to be shown if she came down in your favour. So too with these American officials. They had the power. We had to pander to their every whim. They enjoyed it. We didn't. Once we had demonstrated how in awe of them we really were, the 994 was ours.

So then it was back to the fat one.

"Hi again."

"I Ii."

"Passports."

Assuming that this was a shortened version of "Please could I have your passports," we handed them to him.

"Did you have a nice time in Mexico?"

"Yes thanks."

"Where did you go?"

We started telling him but he would still have nodded if we had said Timbuctoo.

"God, you kids have been everywhere."

Just as we suspected he might have been going for the "Condescending Customs Officer of the Year Award" he spoke again and removed all doubt.

"Now, did you acquire anything in Mexico?"

We felt like telling him we had had lots and lots of lovely presents from Father Christmas, but a man in green uniform with a gun appeared behind him, so we told him we had got some bracelets and Tequila. In fact, we genuinely forgot about the five hammocks, but fortunately a search was not thorough enough to uncover them.

And then, after much more time than it had taken to enter almost every South and Central American country our entry into the "Free World" was finally permitted.

The prohibitive, stark and unfriendly nature of the "Free World" signs continued to strike us:

"Driver has no change."

"For passenger safety Federal Law prohibits operation of this bus while anyone is standing forward of the white line."

The English may be thought over polite, but surely, "Please have the correct change available," and "Please do not stand in front of the white line" get the message across but in a more user-friendly manner.

The signs continued once we had got moving:

"No parking any time."

"Do Not Enter."

"Don't Walk."

"No Parking: Bus Stop."

It was not just the words that hit you, but the size of the signs; they dominated an area far greater than that in which the given activity was forbidden.

All the other signs were big too – big, bold, colourful and presumably an extension of the owner's ego. So struck by them was I that I wrote them down, all of them coming in the first five minutes of the bus ride: "CARL'S HAMBURGERS"; "ALI'S BARBER SHOP"; "FRANK'S SHOE REPAIR"; "DUNKIN' DONUTS";

"YUM YUM DONUTS"; "AUNT EMMA'S PANCAKE RESTAURANT"; "JOE'S AUTOBODY".

Ali had a rival: "BARBERS SHOP REG HAIRCUT $4". How unusual, we thought, for the name of a shop to incorporate its price. It did however leave questions unanswered; was it Reginald's Shop and if so was it only if Reginald himself cut your hair that it cost $4? Or did it perhaps mean registered, which would give it the edge on poor Ali who presumably was not. The only other option I could think of was that it meant "regular", but the idea that anyone would want an irregular haircut led me to discount it.

San Diego was less than an hour's bus ride from the border. Karen, in typical fashion, dashed out between meetings to collect us, and deposited us at the "Museums of San Diego" in Balboa Park. Never before had we seen such a collection of museums in one venue. There was a museum of Photography, of Mankind, of World Folk Art, of Contemporary Art and of the Marines to name just a few. It deserved a day but unfortunately it didn't get it from us.

Karen took us to La Jolla, a delightful sophisticated suburb where environmentalists and historians are fighting to save some of the original, and very stylish, wooden houses from the grasping hands of developers.

San Diego has a high Mexican population, and the Spanish influence could certainly be seen in its architecture. There were spacious and grand houses on the hills around the city from which wealthy owners could enjoy a view of the coastline, and, less enticing, could also see "downtown".

Downtown seemed modern, colourful and cosmopolitan. We dined on Japanese sushis and sukiyaki and owe Karen an expensive meal when she is next in England.

Like any city, however, San Diego has its problems. In particular, drug use (and abuse) is rife and it has a high number of homeless people, on account, Karen explained, of its warm climate and California's relatively easy going, benevolent attitude towards them.

It was a treat to have the luxury of a home, if only for a night, and we had our first taste of a high pressure American shower – where can you get showers like that in England? – and of the sheer

175

size of everything: the enormous fridge, the two dozen egg boxes, the half gallon milk carton . . . they don't do things by halves these Americans. I just wish the process of entering their country could have been toned down a little.

Chapter 45

"I DID NOT OFFICIALLY EXIST for my first two months in California," Pete explained. "Until I got my Californian driving licence, I was a non-person. My passport was not good enough, I couldn't be paid and I couldn't be registered for gas, electricity and so forth."

Pete and I had shared what could even generously only be described as a hut for four months on a Kibbutz in Israel in 1981, both of us having taken a "Year Off" (the first of several in my case) between school and university. England is not well endowed towards scientists and so Pete had taken a job in the States and had been there for one and half years.

It was over an hour's drive from San Diego to Irvine. Much of Southern California is desert, but we stopped off along the way and saw some dramatic coastline reminiscent of Cornwall, frozen yogurt stalls detailing all its "healthy" ingredients, blacks and whites enjoying games of basketball and volleyball together, surfers, BMWs, Pontiacs and lots of Japanese cars, organised barbeque sites and an awful lot of young, tanned, posey Americans.

Following the inevitable and wonderful high pressure shower, we went off to an American institution: an "Eat as much as you want" establishment. After helping ourselves to plates of meat, salad, hot and cold dishes, soup and cheeses, a fresh faced young man came bounding enthusiastically to our table: "Hi, I'm Ben and I'll be serving you tonight," which, given that we had all already served ourselves, caused some confusion.

"How are you all enjoying your Saturday night?" he asked us later.

"Very much thank you, and we hope to continue to if you can leave us alone," we were half tempted to say, but, annoying though this over-zealous attention was, it did not seem right to mock him.

Although Irvine is some 30 miles from Los Angeles city centre and although it was a Sunday we soon hit traffic on our first journey there and crawled the rest of the way.

The first stop was Hollywood. It is a mere shadow of its former self, far removed from the pre-war heyday. Now it is seedy, and we saw several people who looked as if they were drop-outs.

The only vaguely interesting sight we saw was the outside of the Chinese Theatre where the footsteps and handprints of "stars" of several generations are imprinted. Apparently, it was started by accident in the 1930's and has continued ever since. So you can, if you are interested enough, see the prints of the likes of Sylvester Stallone, Elizabeth Taylor and Shirley Temple (taken when she was a child.)

By a large quirk of coincidence, and the minimum of planning, we met Jo's family's neighbours who were holidaying there. It was our first link with home on the whole trip, and it was wonderful to see them. Enjoying a Mau Tei and then a buffet lunch with them in a relatively luxurious Los Angeles hotel, South and Central America seemed ridiculously far away.

It was as if our lives had been put on hold for five months, and now were restored to normality. We talked about the trip as if it was part of history, which in a way it was, and yet this time three days ago we were still on the way to Tijuana.

With the contentment that the combination of alcohol, abundant food, a relaxed setting and good company tends to induce, we were in the mood for two things; further luxury and a bit of exercise.

"Does Beverley Hills appeal?" Pete asked.

"That would do very nicely."

A telephone directory of the residents of Beverley Hills would read like an *International Who's Who?* Literally hundreds of "stars" live in or just off Sunset Boulevard. To be more accurate, they have houses there. They may not necessarily spend much time in them; many apparently have homes in Malibu as well.

178

They were very individual. Raquel Welsh's was notably open and appeared relatively modest, whilst many others were barely visible behind high walls, that of Sammy Davis Junior, who had just passed away, being one of them. The streets were on an incline, and quite windy, and most properties would, I imagine, provide good views over the city. As I write, the Los Angeles riots have not long been over, and I seem to recall reading an article, which struck me as being in extremely bad taste, by a lady who invited her friends to her home in Beverley Hills where they would watch the "fireworks" from the safety of her balcony.

"You'll never get a lift from Irvine," Pete told us (and he had done some hitch-hiking in his time), "I'll take you to a truck stop north of the city."

We set off at 6.10 am. By 7.00, we were in the traffic jam that would lead all the way into the city. The sooner our MP's realise that traffic expands to meet the roads built for it, the better. England will have several Los Angeles on its hands unless it realises very quickly that money must be spent on public transport not roads.

An encouraging sign in an otherwise depressing journey was that one lane was set aside only for people carrying passengers. Now there's an incentive to car-share.

Our first lift was with a truck driver. Jo was dubious about him, but I thought he was OK. Shortly after we had clambered into the back, he pulled a curtain across the window "so the police won't see you, insurance problem."

He was from a little village in Texas and the little he said was fast and barely comprehensible. "You're a long way from home."

"Yeah, I'm often a week from home. I sleep in the truck, now and again in a motel."

He took us within a few hours of San Francisco. It was a flat route on the whole, the land was dry and brown-green in colour, there were some crops – corn, peanuts – and a few orchards. California's reputation for fun and excitement must, we thought, be founded on its coastline. This inland route was certainly sadly devoid of either.

A girl gave us a short lift, time enough only to establish what she did for a living – "I cut hair". I had never heard anyone say that before; even people who do have always described themselves as

179

hairdressers. We wondered if this was an American trait: would a policeman asked the same question say: "I catch criminals", a surgeon: "I cut people up", and a boxer: "I hit people"? Maybe, but I doubt if there's a Los Angeles policeman who would answer by saying: "I beat up blacks in self defence".

Finally, an Indian who had come to the States with some friends to "make good", and appeared to have succeeded took us into central San Francisco.

It was a shock on arriving in San Francisco to see the number of apparent drop-outs sitting around in the streets. They looked OK physically, but they were very scruffy and unkempt, and some were begging. We went for frozen yogurt, and encountered some members of the San Francisco gay community.

San Francisco is historically a "free and easy" city. It was, in the early 1900's, a city of vice: gambling, drinking and prostitution were rife. Whilst it has cleaned up enormously, and is physically an attractive city, it still retains a reputation for tolerance and benevolence to all.

After the pollution, noise and traffic of Los Angeles, it was a Godsend to wander its streets, breathe its air, look out over its Bay, explore its Chinatown and travel on its trams (there's another idea for our cities), and its wonderful spotlessly clean metro system known as BART.

We would depart San Francisco in better spirits, and with more reluctance, than when we had departed Los Angeles.

Chapter 46

OUR FIRST LIFT on the 500 mile journey to Eugene in Oregon progressed us half an hour, but to a worse position. Sometimes, when hitch hiking, it is wise to forego a short lift if you are well positioned. This was such an occasion. Unfortunately by the time we had realised it, it was too late.

It was 15 minutes before we saw another car, but to our surprise and relief it stopped. I asked the young driver if he was heading north. This met with a blank look.

"I do not speak English," he explained in a Spanish accent.

"Espagnol?"

"Si."

We had expected Mexicans in San Diego and Los Angeles, but certainly had not thought that we would find ourselves speaking Spanish north of San Francisco. He was a farm labourer who had come to the States four years ago to learn English. We concluded that either he must have a poor teacher or he hadn't got started yet. The lift was short, but a good one; to a truck stop.

It was lunchtime and we would do well to make Eugene tonight, we thought. We spoke to one "truckie" but an insurance problem prevented him taking us. It was a blessing in disguise: Jenny, going from Berkeley to Portland for a job interview, would take us all the way to Eugene if we could just chip in a bit for the petrol.

Fortunately, her company was good, for the first 200 miles or so were flat and dull, a few trees, some cotton, nuts and fruit presenting only a modicum of interest. However, a dramatic improvement occurred as Oregon approached and we travelled among lovely scenery of lakes and mountains, far more attractive than anything we had yet seen in California.

Once the border was crossed, the Douglas Firs for which the State of Oregon is renowned, appeared in abundance: it was expansive, lush, hilly landscape and we could see mountains in the distance

Our reason for visiting Eugene was because Bob and Zosia were living there. I was fortunate enough to have spent two of my University years in Bob's company; we had engaged very occasionally in intellectual conversation, more often in protracted tussles on the squash court and by far the majority of our time carrying out extensive research into Norwich's abudant supply of public houses. Indeed it was Bob who introduced me to the delights of real ale, and for that, and for a few other reasons, I remain always in his debt. When he had the good sense and good fortune to marry Zosia, there was never any doubt that I had gained, not lost, a friend.

It was an idyllic four days. They had been in Eugene for two years and whilst not considering it wildly exciting, had selected a few choice venues for us, the first of which, appropriately enough, was a bar. I doubt if there is a pub in England like it. Firstly, it looked more like a house than a bar, secondly it was constructed mainly from wood (such is its availability and cheapness) and thirdly it actually had a "drinks menu" – a waitress comes round, takes your order and brings your beer – in our case in three pint pitchers – to the table.

One day, we drove out through "Douglas Fir Country" to two lovely waterfalls and a lake surrounded by forest and mountains which become snow capped in the winter. On another, we visited the remarkably unspoiled Oregon coastline and had a beach to ourselves as we body surfed to our heart's content. You had to keep moving: even with wetsuits, the water was very cold.

We ate out, far more inexpensively than you generally could in England, and we ate in. It was very apparent why there was a generally healthier look to Bob, the married man, than there had been to Bob, the bachelor. Gone were the days when he would suffer apparently inexplicable dizziness on the squash court only for us to then discover that, bereft of any desire to cook, he had eaten one sandwich all day.

On the morning of our departure, I was reminded that, even with marriage and financial advancement, some things never change: Bob's car would not start.

It took 16 hours and 11 lifts to reach Vancouver. This included passing through Portland, Seattle and the Canadian customs, whose employees were as laid back, friendly and quick as the Americans had been uptight, aggressive and painfully slow.

I had met Sacha, who we were visiting, in Burma. In 1987, you were only allowed into Burma for seven days, and the only way to enter and leave was via Rangoon Airport (or at least officially it was). Since almost everybody wanted to visit Mandalay and Pagan, you were always bumping into the same fellow travellers. This detracted somewhat from the concept of exploration and discovery, there being little more crushing to the pioneering spirit than to have hordes of others doing exactly the same thing.

Sacha was someone I was very happy to bump into, and indeed we had even shared a bed in a hostel in Bangkok, although it was sufficiently large for two to sleep in without ever coming into physical contact and it enabled us both to save some ridiculously low amount of money. My nocturnal habits cannot have been too off-putting, for she had visited Jo and me in Bath and here we were spending our final few days in her always interesting company.

I am not sure that we could have had a better finale, nor that there is a modern city anywhere to rival Vancouver.

You can be on the beach in the morning, ski in the afternoon and enjoy the cultural and gastronomic delights of a cosmopolitan city at night. You can pop over to Vancouver Island, you can sail, you can play tennis – there seemed to be courts everywhere – parks were plentiful and we were struck by the number of joggers and cyclists and always, or almost always, you were enjoying wonderful views of the Bay and the mountains.

We were struck also by the apparent cleanliness of the air. Traffic seemed remarkably light; we either walked or took the very efficient electric buses. It seemed that many lived near enough to walk to work, and that those who lived the other side of the Bay to the city centre could travel into work by boat.

At Sacha's suggestion, we visited Granville Island. It is not really an island at all, in that you can walk onto it. It is, however, an area of Vancouver distinct both physically and in nature from the rest, and that perhaps justifies the name. It was once a large industrial region, but had become run down, dirty and smelly. Then a fire damaged it and signalled its end.

In the 1970's a decision was taken to rejuvenate it. The buildings that had previously housed small factories and businesses still stood, and, although they were constructed from corrugated iron and by no means attractive, it was decided to use what was left rather than to knock them down and start from scratch.

It is now a hive of activity; small speciality shops, art galleries, sculptors at work, an Information Centre showing a video of the Island and it even has its own brewery, which obtains its ingredients from Germany. As in the city, you could stroll without being permanently aware of traffic: most people walked, and the few cars were moving very slowly and carefully. The walker, it seemed, had priority.

Walking back into the city centre, we asked a fairly elderly gentleman where we might obtain a map. He said he thought he had a spare one if we could accompany him to his car. Then he offered to drive us to Stanley Park which he told us we must see. This is not the sort of thing which is supposed to happen in cities, we thought – villages perhaps, but cities surely not. As he said it would, the Park had lovely views of the Bay, and how wonderful to see 1,000 acres or so of what would be prime site space devoted solely to a park. Both it, and he, typified a city which neither of us will ever forget.

Chapter 47

IT HAD TO END SOMEWHERE. Vancouver may have left us hankering for more and sad to finish, but it did not. If anything, the reverse applied. If it is good to stop when you are on top, as I believe it is, then we could not have finished on a higher note. To continue would surely have been to go downhill, to detract from the magic of Vancouver and to leave us ultimately feeling deflated.

We had a drunken final night with Sacha in an Irish bar in Seattle, and just about staggered onto the plane the next morning. The flight was awful. We had been told it would be, having booked with TWA, but it was the cheapest and our money had run dry. The scrambled eggs for breakfast were rubbery and inadequate, and there was then a horrendously long wait at the appalling JFK Airport. We had no American dollars and could not change our Canadian money because it was in the form of coins. We were expected to last some nine hours without food. Since I find it impossible, except when asleep, to last more than a few hours without eating, this had all the makings of a disaster.

I recall pleading with a TWA official for something, a pint of milk, anything, but to no avail. Then I recall having no idea how to get back to Jo. And then I recall coming round, Jo virtually force feeding me with milk and bananas scrounged from someone who had originally thought I must be on drugs. It was an unceremonious way to finish. And how ironic, that despite the jabs and pills and the warnings of disease and danger it was not until the finishing straight, in "civilised" America, that either of us would suffer physical breakdown.

This, and the drab, dingy June English weather conspired to put a bit of a dampener on our return. People asked us if we had had a good holiday, generally wanting the whole thing summarised in a few, preferably short, sentences, and told us all about the Poll Tax. We were surprised by the speed of our return to normality.